ECONOMIC COMMISSION FOR LATIN AMERICA AND THE CARIBBEAN

ECLAC

PRELIMINARY OVERVIEW OF THE ECONOMIES OF LATIN AMERICA AND THE CARIBBEAN 1998

UNITED NATIONS

CEPAL
ECLAC

Santiago, Chile, 1998

LC/G.2051-P
December 1998

The *Preliminary Overview of the Economies of Latin America and the Caribbean* is prepared annually by the Economic Development Division in collaboration with the Statistics and Economic Projections Division, the ECLAC subregional headquarters in Mexico and Port of Spain and ECLAC national offices in Argentina and Brazil.

Notes and explanation of symbols

The following symbols have been used in the tables in this *Preliminary Overview*:

Three dots (...) indicate that data are not available or are not separately reported.

The dash (–) indicates that the amount is nil or negligible.

A blank space in a table means that the item in question is not applicable.

A minus sign (-) indicates a deficit or decrease, unless otherwise indicated.

A full stop (.) is used to indicate decimals.

A slash (/) indicates a crop year or fiscal year, e.g., 1969/1979.

Use of a hyphen (-) between years, e.g., 1960-1970, signifies an annual average for the calendar years involved, including the beginning and the end years.

References to "tons" mean metric tons, and to "dollars" United States dollars, unless otherwise stated.

Unless otherwise stated, references to annual growth rates of variation mean cumulative annual rates.

Figures and percentages in tables may not neccessarily add up to the corresponding totals, because of rounding.

UNITED NATIONS PUBLICATION
Sales No. E.98.II.G.15
ISSN 1014-7802 ISBN 92-1-121233-2

CONTENTS

Page

ABSTRACT

The Latin American and Caribbean region will remember 1998 as one of the most problematic years of recent times. The severe effects of the international financial crisis that broke out in Asia in mid-1997 restricted the region's access to external financing. Tumbling export prices translated into the first drop in the value of the countries' exports to be recorded so far this decade, and this in turn led to a further deterioration in the current account of the balance of payments. Faced with this bleak outlook on the external front, economic authorities displayed a strong determination to confront the crisis head on and to build confidence by applying tough monetary, fiscal and exchange-rate policies.

The year's events also included adverse weather conditions on a perhaps unrivaled scale. First there was El Niño, which affected the entire region. Then came a series of hurricanes that ravaged a number of Central American and Caribbean countries.

In view of these upheavals, the economies of Latin America and the Caribbean performed reasonably well, especially considering the fact that macroeconomic policy was primarily focused on achieving and maintaining stability. Nonetheless, the average growth rate for the region was halved, falling from 5.2% to 2.3%. Unemployment rose, although moderately, while the region's average inflation rate leveled off at slightly over 10%. Prudent policy management enabled the region to avoid the turbulent sorts of exchange-rate adjustments experienced by some of the emerging Asian economies in 1997 and by Russia in 1998. Be that as it may, an important conclusion to be drawn from this eventful year is that, all the virtues of the decade's structural reforms and macroeconomic policy measures notwithstanding, the region has made little progress in reducing its external vulnerability.

REGIONAL PANORAMA

1. INTRODUCTION

In 1998 the Latin American and Caribbean countries had to deal with an extremely high degree of volatility in international finance and trade. Considering the strength of the negative external shocks that dampened growth and seriously hampered the management of fiscal and external accounts, the region's economies performed reasonably well. This volatility is still in evidence, however, and many of these shocks have a delayed effect. Consequently, the situation at the close of 1998 and the outlook for 1999 remain highly problematic.

The average growth rate was down sharply, from 5.2% in 1997 to 2.3% in 1998, but even so the rate was higher than the figure for the world economy as a whole, which is estimated at less than 2%. These figures are annual averages, however, and therefore do not reflect the intensification of economic problems that occurred as the year drew on. The typical pattern in most cases was high growth rates during the first six months, owing to the inertia of the 1997 economic expansion, but very slow growth or even contractions during the last two quarters. Employment figures followed a similar trajectory, with the regional unemployment rate holding fairly steady during the first half of the year but climbing during the second. The strongest aspect of the region's performance was in the area of inflation, which has leveled off at around 10% during the past two years, the lowest rate since 1949. The current account deficit widened substantially, jumping from US$ 64 billion in 1997 to US$ 84 billion in 1998, at the same time that capital inflows dropped from US$ 80 billion to US$ 62 billion. Thanks to the region's high level of international reserves, however, it was able to cover its overall US$ 22 billion balance-of-payments deficit (most of which was accounted for by Brazil). It is important to note, however, that long-term capital inflows were nearly as high as their 1997 record level; it was short-term flows that fell.

Interestingly, the types of problems that were experienced in 1998 and their implications differed significantly across subregions. For reasons that varied from one country to the next, South America was especially hard hit. In most cases, with the important exception of Brazil, these countries' export prices were sharply lower, and in Chile and Peru the effects of this downswing were compounded by the loss of Asian markets. On the financial side, a number of the South American countries (especially Brazil, Argentina and Chile) have well-developed stock markets that provide a vulnerable flank for international volatility. In addition, the spillover from the troubled Brazilian economy has been especially problematic in the Southern Cone.

In contrast, Mexico and Central America were able to take advantage of the United States' booming economy to increase the volume of their exports to that country. Furthermore, in a departure from the trend for the region as a whole, which registered a deterioration in its imports/exports price ratio, most of the Central American nations' terms of trade were better than they

LATIN AMERICA AND THE CARIBBEAN: MAIN ECONOMIC INDICATORS

	1996	1997	1998[a]
Economic activity and prices			
Annual rates of variation			
Gross domestic product	3.6	5.2	2.3
Per capita gross domestic product	1.9	3.5	0.7
Consumer prices	18.4	10.3	10.2
Terms of trade	-0.9	3.8	-4.1
External sector			
Billions of dollars			
Exports of goods and services	296.5	327.4	327.3
Imports of goods and services	304.4	359.0	377.7
Balance on goods	6.0	-12.3	-32.9
Balance on services	-13.9	-19.4	-17.5
Balance on income account	-43.1	-46.8	-49.8
Balance on current account	-36.7	-63.7	-83.9
Balance on capital and financial account	62.4	80.4	62.3
Overall balance	25.8	16.8	-21.6
Total disbursed external debt	627.0	650.0	697.8

Source: See statistical appendix.
[a] Preliminary estimates.

had been in 1997. Although various Central American and Caribbean countries sustained severe damage as a result of the hurricanes that ravaged the subregion in the closing months of the year, the brunt of the storms' economic impact will not be felt until later. Since Mexico has much the same type of economic structure as the South American countries, it was also hurt by the year's financial shocks, but thanks to its geographical location in the northern hemisphere, its economy turned in a somewhat better growth performance than the South American countries did.

This all demonstrates that, even though the region has weathered the international crisis fairly well, the depth of the problems facing Latin America and the Caribbean should not be underestimated. The region's

external vulnerability, about which ECLAC has expressed increasing concern in recent years, continues to manifest itself in both the trade and financial spheres. Export prices remain very low, and the possibility that reserves may fail to rebound cannot be ruled out. The cost of financing the countries' growing current account deficits is very high, since the spreads over industrialized countries' interest rates for bond issues have widened by several points while stock market values have tumbled.

At the same time, the Governments face difficult decisions in connection with their macroeconomic goals, since they must choose between raising interest rates in order to protect their exchange rates and guard against any setbacks in terms of inflation, thus slowing the growth of output and employment, or devaluing the currency in order to maintain international competitiveness, which heightens the risk of inflation, adds to the external debt-service burden and may drive down real wages. In practice, so far the majority of the Governments have chosen the first option.

Projections for 1999 suggest that the difficulties of the second semester of 1998 are likely to continue, at least into the first half of the new year. Austerity measures to deal with deficits on the fiscal and/or external accounts will leave little room for expansion, although those Governments that opt for large devaluations –with all the risks they imply– may be able to stimulate their economies through increased exports. Overall, ECLAC estimates suggest that growth for the year will only be around 1%, while inflation should stay in the single digits in the majority of the countries.

The accuracy of these estimates will depend to a great extent on events in the international economy, which are, of course, difficult to project in today's volatile economic context. The performance of the United States and European economies is a key variable that is influenced by a range of different factors about which there is considerable uncertainty (such as the future direction of monetary policy and the behaviour of the relevant stock markets, to cite just a few examples). Moreover, further problems in Asia cannot be ruled out, and the fate of the Brazilian economy will be an especially important factor for the other members of Mercosur. Even under the best of circumstances, a recovery is unlikely to begin before late 1999.

2. MACROECONOMIC POLICY

The general orientation of macroeconomic policy in 1998 has been towards renewed austerity. There are at least two reasons for this. First, there are the effects of the Asian crisis and its intensification in the second half of the year after Russia devalued the rouble and declared a partial moratorium on its foreign debt. Faced with investors' new doubts about risk in emerging markets, the Latin American Governments (with only a few exceptions) decided to send out a clear signal that their priority was to be exchange-rate stability and, hence, austerity.

Another related factor was the widening of external disequilibria; this process had been under way for several years, but it worsened substantially as a result of the negative terms-of-trade shock of 1998. Markets were also less willing to finance these deficits, and the small amount of credit that was available became increasingly expensive, with no signs of a quick return to the falling rates and abundant credit that characterized most of 1997.

Thus, there have been two turning points in recent macroeconomic policy. The first was the sharp change in course made in October 1997 when the Asian crisis began to have its first serious ramifications in Latin American financial markets, and some of the Governments began to adopt preventive monetary and fiscal policies. In other countries, the crisis had a lagged impact on foreign-exchange markets, obliging some of them to adopt a stricter macroeconomic policy stance in early 1998. Fluctuations in international markets –and, in the case of oil-exporters, the drop in oil prices in particular– made it necessary to tighten these adjustment measures still further in the second quarter. The other turning point was marked by the intensification and reinforcement of this new line of economic policy as the international financial crisis deepened in August and September 1998.

Fiscal deficits widen

Despite more cautious policies, the average (unweighted) fiscal deficit for the region increased by one percentage point to 2.4% of GDP in 1998 (see figure 1). Although this is still quite low when compared to the figures for the 1980s, it is the highest to be recorded so far this decade. The main cause of this increase was a decline in current revenue due to slower growth. The fairly generalized reduction in tax revenues was accentuated by the slump in commodity prices, especially in the case of the petroleum-exporting countries (Ecuador, Mexico, Trinidad and Tobago, Venezuela) and metals exporters (Chile, Jamaica). At the same time, expenditure was trending upward owing to higher interest rates (Brazil), increased social budgets and higher public-sector wages, the extraordinary expenditures made necessary by natural disasters (El Niño in Peru and Ecuador, hurricanes in the Caribbean and Central America) and social security reforms (Bolivia, Uruguay).

In response to this situation, which had already become evident by the end of 1997, several countries (Argentina, Brazil, Colombia, El Salvador and Venezuela) raised taxes and bolstered their tax collection efforts. As part of a more widespread response, many Governments in the region also began to make adjustments on the expenditure side, chiefly through reductions in spending on infrastructure and other investment outlays. Public-sector employment and current government consumption were also cut in some cases, but the general tendency was to protect social-sector expenditure. Nevertheless, these efforts failed to hold down costs enough to compensate for lower revenue, and in most cases fiscal policy thus failed to play a useful role in cooling domestic demand or in controlling the countries' rising external deficits.

Figure 1
**LATIN AMERICA AND THE CARIBBEAN:
PUBLIC-SECTOR FISCAL BALANCE**
(Percentage of GDP)

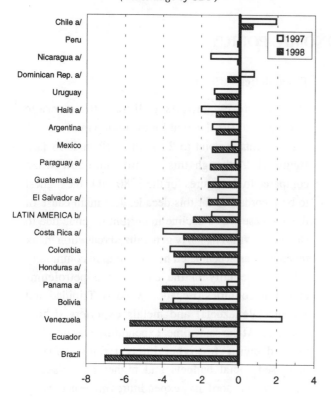

Source: See table A.6 of the statistical appendix.
[a] Central government.
[b] Simple average.

Monetary policy is tightened substantially

Under these circumstances, most of the burden of adjustment fell on monetary policy. The expansion of the money supply and credit facilitated economic growth during 1996 and most of 1997, accommodating the increased demand for local currencies generated by the reconstitution of real monetary balances once their purchasing power had been restored. In October 1997, there was an abrupt change in this trend. After reaching a peak of about 18% in real terms, the growth rate of M1 has been falling steadily ever since. It was almost zero in June and July 1998, and thereafter turned negative. In several countries, the drop in the real money supply reached two digits (see figure 2).

The slower or negative growth of the real money supply during 1998 was attributable to the decrease in foreign assets experienced by most countries in the region. This was not offset by easier domestic credit terms, since interest-rate hikes were used to attract foreign capital and protect the value of the currency when it came under attack. The higher cost of credit was also instrumental in reducing the expansion of domestic demand and in keeping it in line with the slower pace of economic growth.

In terms of the regional average, the year-on-year rise of nominal interest rates that had begun in late 1997 and continued on into the first quarter of 1998 (although they did ease somewhat in some countries, such as Brazil and Argentina) had reached double-digit levels by the third quarter of the year. The interest rate hikes for lending were consistently higher than the increases in rates on deposits, so spreads widened. Real deposit rates, whose across-the-board average was slightly negative at the beginning of 1998 due to seasonal inflation factors, started to climb in April. Decreasing rates of inflation compounded the effect of the nominal rise in interest rates in the second semester, and the region's average real deposit rate as of year's end stood at 10%. In some countries, such as Brazil, real interest rates were much higher.

Overall, monetary policy was successful in cooling down the region's economies (it is expected that the growth of domestic demand will turn out to be negative for the fourth quarter of 1998 in many countries of the region) and in preserving the value of their local currencies. As a consequence of a number of the Governments' decision to rely entirely on monetary instruments in their quest for equilibrium, however, financial costs have reached new highs that may jeopardize future growth prospects. In countries with weak financial sectors, the surge in real interest rates, coupled with slower economic growth, translated into an increase in non-performing loans and a further deterioration of bank assets. Some countries were again hit by banking crises (Ecuador, Paraguay), while others faced greater than expected

Figure 2
**LATIN AMERICA AND THE CARIBBEAN:
MONEY SUPPLY (M1)**
(Real 12-month rates of variation)[a]

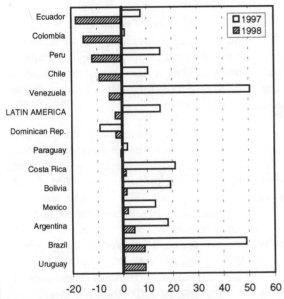

Source: ECLAC, on the basis of official figures.
[a] Most recent period for which data are available; figures deflated by the consumer price index.

difficulties in sorting out the consequences of past ones (Jamaica, Mexico).

Exchange-rate policy becomes controversial

With the tightening of international and domestic credit markets and the resulting slowdown in most economies of the region, the issue of exchange-rate policy became increasingly contentious. Subjects of debate included the exchange-rate regime itself, the use of the exchange rate in stabilization programmes and consistency in the management of semi-flexible systems.

Mounting external deficits drove up the net demand for hard currencies. In general, however, economic authorities did not allow the market to fix parity rates for fear that the climate of widespread uncertainty in international markets might degenerate into uncontrollable devaluations. Financial stability and domestic solvency were also taken into account in defining the acceptable rate of devaluation, as

previous episodes of sustained inflows of external capital and local currency appreciation have left many debtors heavily exposed to exchange-rate risk. Another objective in limiting nominal devaluations was to guard against setbacks in terms of inflation control. This was an especially important motivation in countries that had recently suffered from bouts of high inflation (Brazil, Venezuela).

In these instances the monetary authorities drew on their reserves to forestall excessive devaluations and hiked interest rates to ward off capital flight. Even in Mexico, one of the few economies with a floating exchange-rate regime, the authorities intervened energetically when pressures began to mount at the start of the second semester. In some cases, especially in Brazil, this policy has had two very serious consequences: extremely high interest rates and a loss of reserves. In order to avoid having to modify its exchange-rate regime, Brazil had to request an international rescue package coordinated by the International Monetary Fund (see box 1). Nonetheless, several countries have revised their exchange-rate policies to accommodate currency devaluations, either by altering the floatation band so that the pressure on their currencies can manifest itself in the floating rate, or by increasing the rate of pre-announced devaluations under crawling peg regimes.

The greater control gained over inflation in the region and the increased nominal devaluation rate put an end to the tendency towards appreciation which the average real exchange rate has exhibited for much of the 1990s. In the third quarter of 1998, there were even some signs of a small depreciation in the region, although substantial differences across countries continued to be observed in terms of both exchange-rate movements and their underlying causes (see figure 3).

The Dominican Republic experienced the steepest real depreciation owing to an adjustment in its exchange-rate regime (unification of the official and bank exchange rates) and lower inflation. Paraguay also witnessed a sharp depreciation despite a surge in inflation, but in this case speculative movements in the

Box 1

THE INTERNATIONAL CRISIS AS REFLECTED IN
THE BRAZILIAN ECONOMY

When, on 17 August 1998, Russia announced it was suspending payments on its external public debt for at least 90 days, it triggered renewed uncertainty about emerging countries less than a year after the outbreak of the crisis in Asia. The impact on the Brazilian economy was immediate, as foreign capital fled the country and Brazil found itself without access to new lines of international financing. Between August and October, Brazil's international reserves fell by US$ 27.8 billion to a total of US$ 41.5 billion.

The loss of reserves revealed just how little faith the international market has in the consolidation of the macroeconomic underpinnings of Brazil's economy and in the maintenance of its foreign-exchange policy of controlled, gradual devaluations given recent changes in conditions relating to external financing. The difficulties involved in implementing the fiscal adjustment programme in 1997 and widening deficits on the country's public accounts have raised serious doubts as to the consolidation of the *Real* Plan in view of its excessive dependence on monetary instruments. The Brazilian authorities' initial reaction was to try to distance themselves from Russia's situation by drawing attention to the country's closer ties with the international economy, its stronger production structure and, most importantly, the existence of domestic political conditions that were more conducive to the implementation of the necessary reforms. Another argument that they used had to do with the fact that the price of Brazilian securities on external markets was –thanks to their liquidity– determined primarily by considerations relating to the establishment of hedges against risk on other markets rather than by conditions on the Brazilian market itself. Indeed, in the first few weeks after the outbreak of the Russian crisis, the price of Brazil's leading security, the "C-Bond", dropped by over 20%, thereby signalling a sharp increase in its country risk.

In order to staunch the outflow of resources, the central bank sought to boost earnings from interest-rate arbitrage by doing away with administrative restrictions on foreign capital and lowered the income tax rate on short-term fixed-interest operations for non-resident investors to

zero. Other measures included the increased placement of domestic debt paper that was indexed to the exchange rate or the overnight rate. As a result, the percentage of total securities made up of fixed-interest instruments is estimated to have declined from 41% in January 1998 to around 3% in November.

In the area of fiscal policy, the federal government set a target of 5 billion *reales* for its 1998 primary balance, created a fiscal management commission with legal responsibility for reaching that target figure and announced spending cuts. These measures were not enough, however, and on 10 September the central bank was obliged to raise its rediscount rate from 29.75% to 49.75% per year. The implications of this for the public sector's debt service awakened renewed doubts about the sustainability of fiscal policy. Brazilian capital markets continued to show a great deal of instability throughout September, prompting a steady outflow of capital. The São Paulo stock exchange index dropped nearly 40% during that month, outgoing profit remittances totalled US$ 1.9 billion and the outflow of foreign exchange amounted to US$ 11 billion. External financial markets closed their doors to Brazil. In September it only managed to secure US$ 1.3 billion in loans, compared with a monthly average up to August of US$ 4.7 billion, and the average spread on private bond issues was 776 basis points over United States government bonds.

The outcome of the elections held in early October and the unveiling, towards the end of the month, of a fiscal package designed to increase the primary balance helped to restore calm. This fiscal package paved the way for the development of a plan for the provision of international credit assistance. With the support of the G7, in November the country signed an agreement with the International Monetary Fund concerning a US$ 41 billion financial assistance package put together by the Fund, the World Bank and the Bank for International Settlements. As part of the commitments made by the country in this agreement, it pledged to hold its nominal fiscal deficit in 1999 to no more than 4.7% of GDP, to achieve a primary surplus equivalent to 2.6% and to keep its external deficit to a maximum of 3.5% of GDP (compared to the current 4.2%).

Figure 3
**LATIN AMERICA AND THE CARIBBEAN:
REAL EXCHANGE RATES**
(October 1997-October 1998 variation)

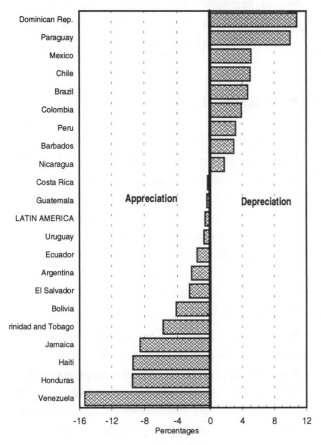

Source: ECLAC, on the basis of official figures.

foreign-exchange market were the cause. Chile and Brazil, on the other hand, succeeded in managing their exchange-rate policy, which included controlled adjustments in a crawling pig regime within a context of lower inflation, in a way that enabled their currencies to regain much of their competitiveness. The same thing occurred in Mexico, which chose to allow some slippage in its floating rate, and in Colombia, which opted for an explicit devaluation of its currency band. At the other extreme, the priority that the Venezuelan authorities placed on controlling inflation prompted them to mount a determined defence of the currency band. Thanks to this policy, which was buttressed by a high level of international reserves, the nominal rate of devaluation was far lower

than inflation. Honduras and Jamaica followed much the same sort of policy, and both of these countries' currencies also appreciated substantially in real terms.

Reforms move forward despite the troubled economic situation

The problematic economic situation existing in 1998 did not seriously affect the structural reform programmes under way in the region. In fact, a record US$ 40 billion in assets were privatized during the year; Brazil led the way, since it accounted for 90% of this figure, with much of that sum being represented by the sale of the national telephone company. A number of the region's smaller economies, including those of Central America, were also very active in this area. The privatization and concession process encompassed a wide range of sectors, including everything from telecommunications to public utilities and postal services. Other areas of reform were the labour market, civil service and pension system.

Trade reforms also moved ahead, with no loss of momentum being noted even in countries troubled by mounting external deficits. Chile, for example, decided to lower its external tariffs in an effort to reach an across-the-board rate of 6% within the next five years and the Central American countries, too, proceeded with their calendar for reducing their level of external protection. On the other hand, employers' associations reacted to the steep slide in the international prices for some products (textiles, steel) with demands for protection against outside competition, and the adoption of protectionist measures by Argentina and Brazil, both members of Mercosur, in such sectors as sugar and motor vehicles impaired trade relations. The issue of whether or not Caribbean banana exports should have special access to the European market continued to divide the countries of the region, despite the reduction made in Caribbean producers' quota.

Despite these sources of friction, the four trade groups in the region –Mercosur, the Andean Community, the Caribbean Community and the Central American

Common Market– continued to make headway with the implementation of their integration agreements. Special emphasis was placed on finding ways to promote convergence among these groups, with Mercosur and the Andean Community taking the lead. The progress made in this respect, however, is still quite limited. As part of another initiative in this field, negotiations were begun at the second Summit of the Americas, held in Santiago, Chile, in April 1998, on a broader, hemisphere-wide agreement with a view to the establishment of the Free Trade Area of the Americas (FTAA) by the year 2005.

3. DOMESTIC ECONOMIC PERFORMANCE

Regional growth slows

The strong expansion in the level of activity seen in the Latin American and Caribbean countries during 1997 –one of the highest growth rates in recent decades– slowed quite abruptly in 1998. The average rate of GDP growth for 1998 is estimated at around 2.3%, more than a full percentage point lower than the average for the 1990s. Output per capita should grow by around 0.7%, putting it nearly 15% above where it was at the beginning of the decade. Because of its size, the Brazilian economy's sluggish growth rate (under 1%) strongly influenced the regional average. Even if Brazil is factored out of the calculations, however, the slowdown still appears to be quite sharp, with the rate falling from 6.6% in 1997 to 3.5% in 1998.

This slowdown in the overall level of activity was due to the results recorded by 13 of the countries in the region (especially Argentina, Peru and Venezuela, where GDP growth was between four and seven points lower) although Venezuela is the only country in which an actual contraction is expected for the year as a whole. Costa Rica was the one country to buck this trend and turn in a substantially better performance than the year before, with a 5% growth rate that was second only to the Dominican Republic's 7%. Quite high growth rates (between 4% and 5%) were reported by nine countries and another three had rates of between 2% and 3% (see figure 4).

The downswing in the region's economies was more serious than the above figures suggest because in many countries it deepened as the year drew on. In the early months of 1998 the economies continued to exhibit the strong dynamism they had shown in 1997, but as the impact of the international financial crisis began to make itself felt through a steep drop in capital inflows and a severe deterioration in the terms of trade, the expansion of output began to flag, coming to a virtual standstill in the final months of the year. The downturn in the terms of trade also affected national income, which is estimated to have edged up by just a little more than 1%.

Investment was a stimulus for growth in most of the countries, since it outpaced GDP. Thus, when measured as a share of output for the region as a whole, this variable showed a slight increase over its 1997 level. Since public-sector investment funds were cut back in many instances as part of the Governments' attempts to control their fiscal deficits, most of the growth in investment came from the private sector, with foreign direct investment (FDI) flows playing a key role in this respect. Consumption expanded at much the same rate as total output, but export volumes were considerably lower than in the past. The volume of imports also grew more slowly than before, but nonetheless continued to outdistance the rate for exports.

The unfavourable conditions observed in 1998 were reflected more clearly in the industrial activity of the countries of the region. The most serious downturn was in Brazil, where industrial output is expected to have dropped by 2.8% after having climbed by over 4% in 1997. The results were also poor in Argentina, where industrial activity slid during the closing months of 1998 following a strong performance early

Figure 4
**LATIN AMERICA AND THE CARIBBEAN:
GROSS DOMESTIC PRODUCT**
(*Annual rates of variation*)

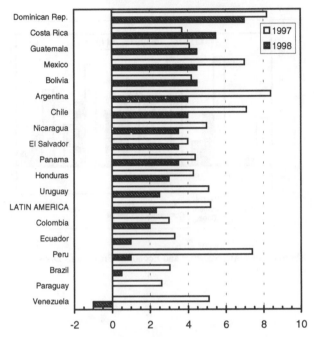

Source: See table A.1 of the statistical appendix.

in the year. The same thing happened in Chile, Colombia and Venezuela, all of which exhibited clearly recessionary trends in the final quarter. Mexico's industrial growth rate also slumped towards the end of the year, but the rate for the first nine months of 1998 was much higher (nearly 8%). Nevertheless, the downward trend is expected to deepen from the fourth quarter of 1998 on. The situation was quite different in Peru, where activity waned in the first two quarters as a consequence of El Niño, which had a particularly serious impact on the production activity of industries that process agricultural and fish products. Activity then rebounded during the second half of the year once these adverse weather conditions came to an end.

Economic activity in a number of countries was adversely affected in 1998 by El Niño, which caused serious droughts and flooding that had a particularly severe impact on agriculture. Fisheries were also hurt by this phenomenon, which did a great deal of damage

to infrastructure as well. In the closing months of 1998 Central America and the Caribbean were hit by two hurricanes that caused an enormous amount of destruction; the full force of the impact that this will have on the level of economic activity will not become evident until 1999, however (see box 2).

The outlook for 1999 is problematic

The economic growth of Latin America is expected to weaken further in 1999 as a result of the continuing international economic crisis and the impact of the adjustment policies that the countries have begun to implement in order to cope with it. The region's export prices will remain low at least for several more months, which will hurt its balance of payments and fiscal accounts. This will make it necessary to proceed with adjustment measures that will constrain economic activity. In some of the Central American and Caribbean countries, these factors will be compounded by the effects of the storms and other adverse weather conditions that affected them during the second half of 1998. These phenomena seriously impaired vital economic activities, and the after-effects are expected to persist for quite some time.

As we have seen, these factors caused the region's economic growth rate to falter during the second half of 1998. Consequently, the new year will be starting out under a cloud, with a number of economies in recession and no signs of a turnaround in the situation any time soon. The region's overall growth rate is projected at just slightly over 1%, with a rate of over 5% being registered by only one country and actual decreases in the level of activity in three of the 19 economies considered. In Brazil, the region's largest economy, GDP may shrink by 1% as a result of the harsh adjustment programme launched by the Government in order to deal with the hefty deficits registered on the country's external and fiscal accounts. A contraction in Venezuela's GDP is also expected owing to the low level of oil prices, which may make cutbacks in public expenditure necessary.

Honduras is expected to see a slump in economic activity as well, since it was hit the hardest when Hurricane Mitch swept through the subregion in November.

Argentina, Chile and Uruguay had posted strong growth rates in 1997 but witnessed an abrupt slowdown in 1998, and this downward trend is likely to persist in 1999. In Colombia, growth is expected to subside for similar reasons. Mexico's economy expanded vigorously for the first three quarters of 1998, but will grow more slowly in 1999 owing to the persistence of high interest rates, sharply lower oil revenues and problems in the banking system. A downswing in the Central American countries' growth rates is likely due, in particular, to the storms and other weather-related factors mentioned earlier, although Costa Rica may once again grow at a reasonably good pace. It is also possible that the Dominican Republic's rapid rate of economic expansion may continue (see figure 5).

Inflation stabilizes at its low 1997 level

After the steep reduction in inflation seen between 1990 and 1997, the regional rate fell only marginally in 1998. In recent years, a dramatic drop had been observed, with inflation plummeting from 882% in 1993 to 335% in 1994, 26% in 1995, 18% in 1996 and 10.3% in 1997. In 1998, the rate for the 12 months to November was 10.2%, the lowest in nearly 50 years. The significance of the average rate is reinforced by the fact that 11 of the 19 countries considered had single-digit inflation rates. Moreover, in the majority of countries the rate fell or remained low; only Ecuador, Nicaragua and Paraguay had significant increases. Although Venezuela reduced its rate from 38% to 31%, this was still high in comparison with the region's current patterns and was exceeded only by Ecuador, where prices rose by 45% (see figure 6).

Argentina continued to maintain its record as best performer, registering near-zero inflation, as it had also done during the two previous years. Brazil

Figure 5
LATIN AMERICA AND THE CARIBBEAN: GDP PROJECTIONS FOR 1999
(Percentages)

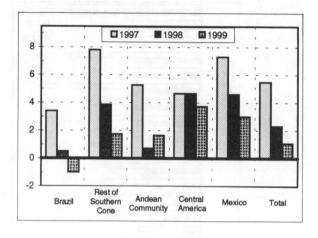

Source: ECLAC, Statistics and Economic Projections Division.

consolidated its control over price increases as, after experiencing four-digit inflation in the late 1980s and early 1990s, its inflation rate in 1998 was only 3%. The biggest advances occurred in the Dominican Republic, Haiti and Uruguay; in the case of Uruguay, the inflation rate may well turn out to have been the lowest since 1957. Currency devaluations were the primary cause of inflation in a number of countries (Ecuador, Nicaragua and Paraguay).

The significant deceleration of inflation in the 1990s has mainly been due to a change in economic policy in recent years. The fight against inflation has come to be the highest priority of macroeconomic policy, and this policy effort worked in conjunction with structural reforms and a promising international environment up until mid-1997. The financial problems affecting the world economy in 1998 have not had strong repercussions on domestic prices. With the exceptions mentioned above, devaluations did not translate into significant price rises, given the restrictive monetary policies and recessionary situation that existed in various countries of the region.

Box 2

THE IMPACT OF NATURAL DISASTERS ON THE REGION'S ECONOMY

The loss of life, economic damage and destruction of productive capital caused by natural disasters have been particularly severe in 1998. The year was marked by two types of natural phenomena in particular –El Niño and hurricanes Georges and Mitch– whose effects will surely continue to be felt in the medium term in view of the amount of time it will take to rebuild the countries' stocks of capital goods and infrastructure.

The region's latest bout with **El Niño**, which began in 1997, included both floods and droughts that caused an estimated US$ 15 billion in damage and production losses. In the Andean subregion alone (Bolivia, Colombia, Ecuador, Peru and Venezuela), the damage is estimated at US$ 7.5 billion. El Niño's main impact has taken the form of diminished income and lower living standards for large groups of people, especially among the poorer sectors of the population.

El Niño caused a great deal of damage in the fishery and agricultural sectors due to the extensive flooding it caused in 1997 and 1998 along the coasts of Peru and Ecuador and in various areas of Argentina, Chile, Brazil and Paraguay. Housing, social infrastructure and production facilities were destroyed or damaged, and production levels were substantially lower in manufacturing, commerce, mining and tourism.

Droughts occurred in large areas of Colombia, Venezuela, Mexico, the Central American nations, a number of Caribbean countries and –at least in 1998– some South American countries. The worst impact of the droughts was in the agricultural sector. Countries that rely on hydroelectric power had to resort to more expensive thermoelectric facilities. In addition, the drought increased the likelihood of fires, resulting in the loss of large tracts of forest land and other types of environmental damage.

Hurricane Georges made its first landfall on the island of Antigua on 20 September. After sweeping over a number of other islands in the Antilles, it continued on a path that took in Puerto Rico, the Dominican Republic, Haiti and Cuba, causing heavy damage (estimated at US$ 1.35 billion in the Dominican Republic and US$ 400 million in Saint Kitts and Nevis).

In late October and early November, Central America was hit by **Hurricane Mitch**, one of the most destructive hurricanes of this century. Mitch left such a wide trail of death and destruction in its path that the magnitude of that damage has yet to be calculated. Honduras was the hardest-hit country. Nearly 6,000 people died and another 300,000 lost their homes, means of livelihood and jobs. In Nicaragua, 19% of the population was affected. Although the damage was less severe in Guatemala and El Salvador, the repercussions are significant because the worst destruction occurred in highly vulnerable areas of these countries.

The damage sustained by the region's infrastructure is considerable, and trade flows among these countries have been interrupted because of the destruction caused in the transport sector. Electrical power generation and distribution capabilities have also been impaired, as have drinking water and sanitation services. The damage to the agricultural sector is estimated at over US$ 2.3 billion. In the manufacturing and services sectors, the direct damage is more limited, but the projected loss of income may depress the level of economic activity in the subregion. Customs-free areas and export processing zones (EPZs) for *maquila* industries do not appear to have sustained a great deal of direct damage, but they have been hurt by short-run disturbances and by the higher cost of some services, such as port transport and shipping.

In summary, preliminary estimates put the direct and indirect losses at over US$ 7 billion, including replacement costs. Nearly 68% of the damage is concentrated in Honduras and another 17% in Nicaragua. The State's response capacity in the face of this emergency has been reduced both by the increased expenditures required to deal with the most urgent needs and by the decrease in tax revenues occasioned by the drop in production. This situation poses major challenges with regard to institution building and fiscal administration. The international community is making a determined effort to help rebuild the subregion and is extending over US$ 6 billion in soft loans for reconstruction projects. Some creditor countries have also offered to forgive portions of these nations' external debts.

Figure 6
**LATIN AMERICA AND THE CARIBBEAN:
CONSUMER PRICES**
(12-month rates of variation)[a]

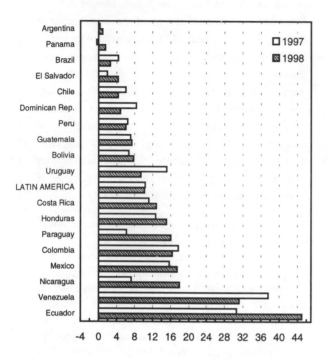

Source: See table A.3 of the statistical appendix.
[a] Most recent period for which data are available.

Labour markets suffer a reverse

The slower rate of economic growth in 1998 translated into higher unemployment, which rose from 7.3% on average for the region in 1997 to 7.9% in 1998. This increase was primarily due to a worsening situation in the labour market in Brazil and Colombia, where unemployment climbed significantly. In contrast, thanks to a relatively rapid pace of growth –even if slower than the year before– the annual average rate of unemployment in most of the countries in the region was stationary or even fell. Sizeable reductions in

joblessness were reported in Argentina, Barbados, Dominican Republic, Mexico, Nicaragua, Trinidad and Tobago, and Uruguay. It is important to note, however, that all of these countries except Mexico still have double-digit unemployment rates (see figure 7).

In the second half of the year, the deceleration of growth in many countries began to be reflected in the labour market. Accordingly, the unweighted average employment rate for the countries having this information available –which had risen sharply in the second half of 1997 and moderately in the first half of 1998– showed a small decline. The weighted average employment rate exhibited a different trend, with a large decrease in the first part of the year and a small upswing in the second; this was mainly due to the influence of Brazil, where this latter pattern predominated.

Overall, the employment rate was down. Specifically, the demand for labour weakened in various parts of the formal sector that were hurt by external problems and by adjustment measures; this is what occurred, for example, in Chile's mining, forestry, fishery and construction industries. In some of the countries ravaged by natural disasters, jobs were lost in agriculture, as in the case of Honduras' banana plantations. Most countries saw a reduction in employment in manufacturing as a consequence of the more sluggish growth of domestic demand, external competition and labour-saving restructuring plans. As a result, in many cases job creation was concentrated in the informal sector of the economy in 1998. In some countries, however, such as Mexico, economic buoyancy also led to the creation of a significant number of formal-sector jobs.

In the context of a slacker demand for labour, real wages in the formal sector stagnated or fell slightly in most countries. In fact, of the countries having information available, only Chile and Uruguay registered increases of more than 1%.

4. THE EXTERNAL SECTOR

The current account deficit continues to widen

The combined effects of an international financial crisis and a series of weather disasters were reflected in the deteriorating position of the external sector in the majority of the countries. Thus, the trend towards widening current account deficits intensified. The aggregate regional deficit rose from 2% of GDP in 1996 to over 3% in 1997 and topped 4% in 1998, although the latter percentage was skewed upward by the devaluation of many of the countries' currencies, which lowered the value of GDP measured in dollars. The current account deficits were close to the regional average in the three largest economies (Argentina, Brazil and Mexico), but reached levels around or above 7% of GDP in Chile and the Andean countries other than Venezuela (see figure 8).

The increased current account deficit for Latin America and the Caribbean in 1998 was due to the marked deterioration in the trade balance, since factor services did not change much. Although profit remittances continued to expand, interest payments

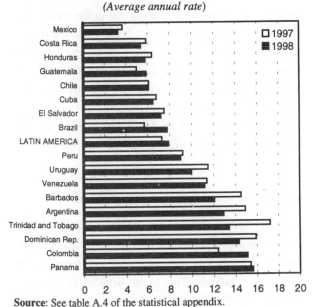

Figure 7
LATIN AMERICA AND THE CARIBBEAN: URBAN UNEMPLOYMENT
(Average annual rate)

Source: See table A.4 of the statistical appendix.

increased little. In contrast to 1997, in 1998 the region had to resort to international reserves and compensatory capital in the amount of nearly US$ 22 billion to finance the current account deficit. The decline in reserves was particularly marked in Brazil, Chile and Venezuela, somewhat less so in Colombia and Peru. On the other hand, some countries did increase reserves, notably Argentina and Mexico.

Although the trend towards deteriorating current accounts and trade balances continued, the reasons for it changed radically from previous years. Whereas in recent years the import-export gap was due to a surge in imports, in 1998 it was due chiefly to a weakness in exports.

Exports slacken

The value of regional merchandise exports declined for the first time in twelve years. The contraction of over 1% compared to the previous year was due to a sharp drop in prices, which was only partially offset by a growth in export volumes less dynamic than the previous year's.

The unit value of the region's exports declined on average by more than 8%. This reflected the sharp drop in commodity prices in world markets, which were heavily influenced by the financial crisis that erupted in Asia during the second half of 1997. Prices of raw materials, from both mining and agriculture, were particularly affected. The price index average elaborated by ECLAC for the first three quarters of 1998 shows a decline with respect to the previous year of 15% in prices of minerals and tropical beverages and more than 10% in the prices of foods and agricultural raw materials. Moreover, during the fourth quarter the prices of many products, particularly petroleum and copper, continued to drop.

The price of oil was halved between October 1997 and December 1998, falling to its lowest level in twelve years. That one fact explains why Venezuela

Figure 8
**LATIN AMERICA AND THE CARIBBEAN:
CURRENT ACCOUNT BALANCE**
(Percentage of GDP)

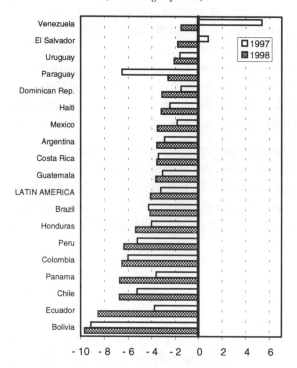

Source: See table A.11 of the statistical appendix.

The majority of the countries were able to make up to some extent for the drop in prices by expanding export volumes, but growth in that respect was less dynamic than in previous years because of the problems importing countries were experiencing. Reduced demand for imports was most evident in the Asian economies, and this seriously dampened export sales for Chile and Peru in particular. Also a factor was the economic slowdown in some other countries, such as Brazil, an important market for many Latin American exporters. The good performance of the United States economy, by contrast, benefited Mexico in particular as a member of the North American Free Trade Agreement (NAFTA). Overall, United Nations estimates indicate that the growth the world economy slowed by half in 1998 and should turn out to be under 2%. Growth in world trade similarly slowed, according to the World Trade Organization, and should be between 4% and 5%, roughly half of the growth rate for 1997.

On the other hand, preliminary figures suggest that exports of manufactures were the best performers in some countries of the region and helped to soften the impact of the declines in primary commodities, which make up the bulk of the region's exports. These differing trends are consistent with indications that exports to other markets within the region again grew more rapidly than exports to the rest of the world. The data so far available suggest a clear tendency in that direction within the Andean Community and the Central American Common Market, but the trend was halted in the case of Mercosur by the impact of the cooling of the Brazilian economy on the exports of its neighbours (see box 3 for a description of the interrelationships between the Mercosur economies).

Imports slow and terms of trade worsen

Imports slowed throughout the region as domestic demand weakened and the currencies of many of the countries, for the first time in several years, underwent real depreciation. The most drastic adjustment occurred in Brazil, nearly the only country where

experienced by far the greatest decline (26%) in export unit value. Ecuador, Chile and Peru suffered declines of between 13% and 14%. The latter two countries were hard hit by the falling prices of metals, particularly copper. In Colombia and Paraguay, the losses were around 10%, while some other countries experienced smaller but still substantial declines. In the Central American countries, export unit values either declined slightly or held stable; banana prices were firm and there was a lag before the drop in the price of coffee was reflected in sale contracts. The Caribbean countries were variously affected: Trinidad and Tobago suffered losses in terms of its exports of hydrocarbons and petrochemical products that amounted to the equivalent of 2% of GDP, while Guyana and Jamaica were hurt by lower prices for bauxite.

Box 3

BRAZIL AS A TRANSMISSION CHANNEL OF MACROECONOMIC SHOCKS TO OTHER MERCOSUR COUNTRIES

Brazil accounts for a large share of the foreign trade of the other Mercosur members. Hence it becomes a channel by which the external shocks that affect it are transmitted. The importance of the Brazilian market in Argentina's foreign trade, for example, has doubled since the start of the decade; in 1997, it accounted for 26% of all Argentine imports and exports. Access to the Brazilian market is also important for Uruguay, which sells one third of its exports to Brazil, covering a wide range of agricultural and industrial products. As for Paraguay, Brazil has bought nearly half of its exports in recent years.

It has been observed that fluctuations in macroeconomic variables in Brazil, once they reach a certain amplitude, tend to have a noticeable impact on its Mercosur partners through bilateral trade. Argentine exports to Brazil are highly sensitive to variations in the Brazilian economy, responding with an average elasticity of 2.5 to changes in GDP. The elasticity of their response to variations in the real exchange rate of Brazil appears to be lower than one, and the effect is by no means negligible when exchange rate fluctuations are substantial. During the 1995 crisis, the stimulus of Mercosur demand was highly important to Argentina, as it partially offset the contractionary effect of the decline in external credit. For Paraguay, the cooling of Brazilian demand in 1998 translated into a 30% decline in its exports to Brazil.

The indirect implications are equally important. The effects of Brazilian demand on Argentina, for example, have repercussions in Uruguay, since Argentina is the second-largest market for its goods and its chief customer for tourist services.

It is true that a sizeable portion of intraregional trade consists of relatively undifferentiated primary commodities that can easily be diverted to other markets with no problems other than additional freight costs. But non-agriculture-based manufactures are also important, and there the situation is different. A prime example is the Argentine motor vehicle industry: the Brazilian market absorbs more than half of its exports. For that group of exports, the alternative foreign markets are more limited, and the industries that manufacture them are more sensitive to the economic cycle.

In addition to transmission by way of trade, there are investment effects. It is likely that a significant proportion of decisions on whether to make capital investments in manufacturing are influenced by expectations regarding the regional market. Nor can the possibility be ruled out that contagion from Brazil affects Argentine financial markets, although external demand for Argentine bonds is still more heavily influenced by factors specific to the country's economy or dependent on the international situation. The early stage of development of markets in private assets in Paraguay and Uruguay keep turbulence in financial markets from having much impact in that sphere. On the contrary, since Uruguay has traditionally played the role of "refuge" or "safe house" for the region's capital, at times of financial uncertainty deposits of non-residents (primarily Argentines) flow into its banking system. However, rumours of a possible devaluation in Brazil in 1998 resulted in greater demand for foreign exchange in Paraguay and a 10% real depreciation of the guaraní.

import volume actually contracted. There, as in the other large economies, the flow of imports remained heavy during the early months of the year, but gradually slackened as the domestic economic situation deteriorated. Growth in import volume for the region as a whole was 11%, considerably less than half the figure for the year before, but similar to that for 1996.

In value terms, the reduction was even greater, as prices of imported products fell significantly throughout the region. One factor was the decline worldwide in prices of manufactures, reflecting lower prices for raw materials and more intense competition due to the devaluation of Asian currencies; at the same time, petroleum and other raw materials imported by the countries of the region became cheaper. As a result, the region's bill for imports only increased by around 6%, after two years of strong expansion. Currency savings were especially significant in purchase of oil and gas; most of the petroleum-importing countries for which information is available paid from 20% to 40% less than the previous year for oil and gas.

The slackening pace of imports was due in part to greater difficulty in financing them, owing to constraints on external borrowing and slower growth of the purchasing power of exports. The latter expanded by only a little over 3% for the region as a whole, owing to a combination of weak growth in export volumes and the deterioration in the terms of trade.

The decline in the region's terms of trade, however, was less than 4%, thanks to the considerably cheaper prices for imports. While roughly half the countries suffered a deterioration in their terms of trade, the other half found that lower prices for their exports were more than offset by lower prices for the products they imported. The chief gainers in this respect were the Central American countries, Uruguay and the Dominican Republic, where the effect of the improvement in the terms of trade was equivalent to around 1% of GDP or more; in the case of Honduras the figure was 3%, in Nicaragua 4%. The chief losers were the exporters of petroleum (Ecuador, Trinidad

and Tobago and, above all, Venezuela) and metals (Chile, Jamaica, Guyana). Terms of trade losses exceeded 5% of GDP in Venezuela and 2% in Chile and Ecuador. In Brazil, the two effects offset one another (see figure 9).

The net aggregate effect of the variation in the terms of trade for the region as a whole was negative and amounted to over US$ 10 billion, equal to nearly half of the international reserves lost by the region in 1998 and to half a percent of the region's GDP for the year.

Capital inflows moderate

The impact of the international financial crisis on capital flows to Latin America, already observable in

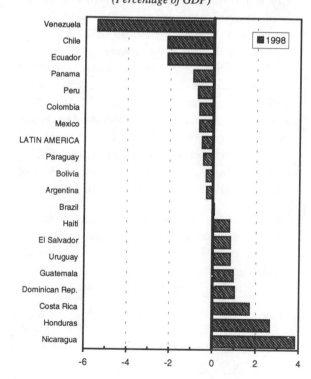

Figure 9
**LATIN AMERICA AND THE CARIBBEAN:
TERMS OF TRADE GAINS AND LOSSES**
(Percentage of GDP)

Source: ECLAC, on the basis of official figures.

some countries of the region in the fourth quarter of 1997, was felt more broadly in 1998, especially from August onward, as the region began to experience the effects of the devaluation of the rouble and Russia's unilateral debt moratorium. In 1998 Latin America received only US$ 62 billion, compared with an influx of US$ 80 billion in 1997 (as a percentage of GDP, a decline from 4.2% to 3.2%). Autonomous capital inflows declined in over half of the Latin American and Caribbean countries. Among those most heavily affected were Brazil, Chile and Peru; Venezuela continued to record a net outflow. Five others, notably Argentina, managed to increase their external financing.

A significant feature of external financing in 1998 was that a large proportion continued to take the form of medium- and long-term funds, especially foreign direct investment. In several countries lending from multilateral organizations assumed greater importance, including some important loan commitments for disbursal in 1999. On the other hand, there were outflows of short-term capital and sharp declines in stock market investment in most of the countries of the region. The latter occurred chiefly between August and October 1998, when substantial short-term capital flight occurred, especially from Brazil.

Net foreign direct investment inflows to the region remained close to the extraordinary level of US$ 57 billion achieved in 1997. In nine Latin American countries, foreign direct investment again financed over half the current account deficit of the balance of payments. The chief beneficiary was Brazil, which received a record US$ 22.5 billion. Much of that amount came from the privatization of the telecommunications system (Telebras), the largest such sale in the history of Latin America. Although flows to Argentina, Chile, Colombia and Mexico slowed, they nonetheless contributed significantly to financing the current account deficit. Also important were the direct investment flows to some Central American and Caribbean countries, notably El Salvador and Guatemala.

Bond issues in the first half of 1998 amounted to US$ 28 billion in gross terms, a figure similar to that recorded in the first half of 1997. Argentina, Brazil, Mexico and Venezuela continued to account for most issues. The cost of external financing did not increase significantly during the first half (see figure 10). Towards the end of August, however, the cost of financing in the secondary market rose considerably to nearly 15% per annum, and has only partially reversed course during the closing months of the year. Because of the higher cost, Governments and companies in the region placed no new bond issues between August and October 1998. It was not until November that the Government of Argentina tested the waters with a bond issue for US$ 1 billion, the first major issue to come out of the region since the international crisis intensified in August; it was followed by an issue for US$ 1.5 million by PEMEX of Mexico.

Bank credit to the region rose by only 5% in the first half of 1998, and loans were concentrated entirely in the first quarter. Since the eruption of the Asian crisis in October 1997, at times syndicated loans have

Figure 10
LATIN AMERICA AND THE CARIBBEAN: INTERNATIONAL BOND ISSUES

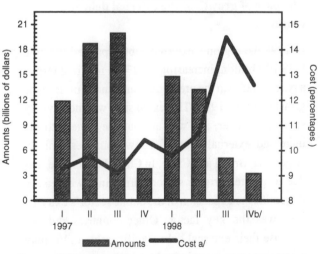

Source: ECLAC, on the basis of official figures and data provided by the World Bank and the International Monetary Fund.
[a] The sum of the average spread on the bond issues plus the yields on long-term United States Treasury bonds.
[b] October to 4 December.

been the only external credit option open to some Latin American countries. Moreover, they have offered better credit terms than bonds. However, syndicated financing has been very selective, available only to a few Governments and companies in the region. Supplier credit, on the other hand, which makes up the greater portion of short-term debt in most of the economies, has continued to be granted as usual.

The international financial crisis depressed stock market prices; between October 1997 and mid-September 1998 the region's stock exchanges all registered declines. During that period, the regional index fell by a cumulative 50%, after several years of gains. Although in mid-September the regional index of stock prices began to recover, by mid-December 1998 it still had not risen above its level at the beginning of 1996 (see figure 11). Thus, foreign investment in stock market assets was one of the flow components most heavily affected during 1998. By September 1998, it had dropped off by US$ 10 billion in the countries of the region for which information is available. One of the elements of stock market investment, issues of American Depositary Receipts (ADRs), which had reached US$ 5 billion in 1997, amounted to practically nothing in 1998.

The pace of growth of the external debt quickens

In 1998 the region's external debt expanded to some US$ 700 billion, increasing by 7% in nominal terms, a pace faster than the previous year's and similar to the growth rate in 1995. The expansion was not evenly spread, however, and was attributable largely to the increased external debt of a few countries, chiefly Argentina, Brazil and Chile. In Chile the increase was due to greater private sector borrowing, whereas in Argentina the expansion of the public sector's external debt was the key factor. Other countries did not increase their external debt significantly, and it may prove that some actually reduced it in nominal terms.

Figure 11
**LATIN AMERICA AND THE CARIBBEAN:
STOCK EXCHANGE PRICES**
(Variation in indices expressed in dollars)

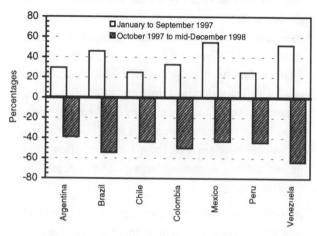

Source: ECLAC, on the basis of figures from the International Finance Corporation.

For the first time in the 1990s, the indicators of the region's external debt burden reflected a turn for the worse, chiefly because of the stagnation in exports of goods and services. For example, the ratio of accrued interest to exports of goods and services rose from 14.5% to 15.5%, and the ratio of the external debt to exports of goods and services rose from 193% to 207%. Although the deterioration was widespread, over half of the countries showed debt indicators still considered acceptable. For the others, especially some of the Central American countries, the indicators continued to grounds for concern (see table A.17).

With regard to external debt renegotiation, in 1998 a debt relief programme went into effect in Bolivia under the terms of the Heavily Indebted Poor Countries (HIPC) debt initiative. Also under that initiative, the International Monetary Fund, the Inter-American Development Bank and the World Bank announced that they were considering the possibility of an external debt relief programme for Nicaragua and Honduras.

SOUTH AMERICA

ARGENTINA

Growth in the level of activity slowed but, for the year as a whole, GDP again increased at an appreciable rate of about 4%. Given the deterioration in the terms of trade and increased outlays in the form of external factor payments, the growth rate for national income (8% in 1997 and 6% on average since the beginning of the decade) fell to 3%. Rising investment was once again a prominent component of expenditure, with fixed capital formation representing about 25% of GDP. Export volumes rose substantially. Output growth was concentrated in the first half of the period, during which the annualized increase exceeded 7%. During the second half of the year, there were signs that both demand and economic activity were cooling off, and seasonally adjusted GDP was lower than in the first six months. The average unemployment rate for 1998 was around 13%, and inflation was again very low (0.9%).

During the early months of 1998, the repercussions of the international crisis were reflected in lower international prices for exports. Since there was a sufficient supply of external funds, however, spending increases were not restricted to any great extent by that variable. During the first half of the year capital inflows were abundant; imports increased, particularly those of capital goods, and international reserves rose. The mood of financial markets changed suddenly in August, however, following the outbreak of the crisis in Russia. Share prices fell to levels below the 1995 average, and the spread in yields between Argentine securities and those issued by industrialized

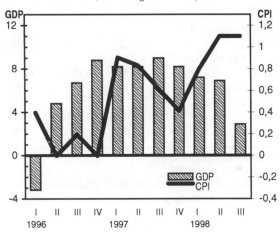

ARGENTINA: GROSS DOMESTIC PRODUCT AND INFLATION
(Percentage variation)

Source: ECLAC, on the basis of official figures.

countries widened. Later, when the tension on international markets eased, the prices of Argentine securities recovered. Credit terms remained tighter than before, however.

Unlike what had occurred in 1995, bank deposits did not contract, although there was some shift away from peso deposits and towards dollar deposits. The banking system, where the participation of foreign entities has grown considerably, still appeared to be free from any appreciable degree of fragility and, most importantly, to have considerable liquidity reserves. Nonetheless, the volume of bank credit stagnated in September and October. Spending on goods and services was curbed by the increase in interest rates

ARGENTINA: MAIN ECONOMIC INDICATORS

	1996	1997	1998[a]
	Annual rate of variation		
Gross domestic product	4.4	8.4	4.0
Consumer prices	0.1	0.3	0.9
Real wages	-0.2	-0.5	-1.2
Money (M1)	11.2	14.7	5.9
Real effective exchange rate[b]	1.9	-2.9	-2.5
Terms of trade	4.4	2.1	-4.5
	Percentages		
Urban unemployment rate	17.2	14.9	12.9
Fiscal balance/GDP	-1.8	-1.4	-1.2
Real deposit rate	7.6	6.6	5.9
Real lending rate	19.5	13.6	12.2
	Millions of dollars		
Exports of goods and services	27 037	29 318	29 450
Imports of goods and services	27 910	34 899	36 650
Current account	-3 787	-9 454	-12 200
Capital and financial account	7 025	12 516	15 200
Overall balance	3 238	3 062	3 000

Source: See the statistical appendix.

[a] Preliminary estimates.

[b] A negative rate signifies an appreciation of the currency in real terms.

and by the cautious attitude which seems to have spread among both lenders and potential borrowers. This also affected external trade flows, with signs being seen of a weakening demand for imports. This helped to hold down the trade deficit, although for the year as a whole it was higher than in 1997.

During the first three quarters of 1998 the public sector's cash deficit remained within the range provided for in the country's agreement with the IMF, but fiscal policy came under pressure in the fourth quarter. The total deficit for the period is estimated at close to 1.1% of GDP, which was somewhat above the target level. The increase in interest payments was offset by a larger primary surplus. This result was achieved, even though revenues rose less than

expected, by reining in increases in expenditure. During the first 10 months, national tax receipts rose less (4%) than output. There was an especially significant increase in revenues from profit and wealth taxes, however, while VAT receipts rose by 3% and social security collections held steady.

Faced with this downturn in revenue, the authorities decided to introduce the prepayment of taxes on income earned in 1998. The Government also proposed various reforms of the tax structure, including modifications in the profit tax and the extension of the VAT to previously exempt activities. A system specifically designed for small taxpayers came into force in October under which income taxes, VAT and social security contributions were all consolidated into a single tax.

In the area of finance policy, it had been the Government's practice to programme issues of debt instruments ahead of the corresponding funding requirements. When the demand for government bonds contracted, the authorities were therefore able to refrain from floating any more debt paper without suffering from acute liquidity problems. When the bout of financial turbulence subsided, the Government began to issue bonds again.

Monetary policy remained focused on the behaviour of the financial system. There were increases in deposit insurance coverage and in the amount of stand-by credits available to the central bank should the need arise to provide liquidity to the nation's banks. The system as a whole did not fall prey to the problems experienced by a number of medium-sized institutions which were forced to suspend operations.

After much debate, labour reforms were passed which enjoy the support of the trade unions but not of employers' organizations. The new legislation lowers severance payments somewhat and eliminates certain types of fixed-term employment contracts whose use had been on the rise.

During the first half of the year the level of activity climbed rapidly as investment boomed (18%) in construction and, especially, in machinery and equipment. Consumption grew at a much slower but still appreciable rate (over 5%). The 1997/1998 grain harvest exceeded 65 million tons; this was 23% more than in the previous crop year, which itself had set an all-time record. In addition to favourable weather conditions, this result was due to the expansion of the area under cultivation and improvements in farming methods. Nonetheless, producers' decisions concerning the area to be planted for the 1998/1999 grain crop were influenced by the trend in international prices. In manufacturing, the first half of the year saw considerable increases in the output of motor vehicles, home appliances, construction materials and other intermediate goods such as iron and steel and chemicals. There was a significant increase in activity in public utilities as well, particularly communications and certain areas of the transport sector.

The downturn in activity in the last months of the year was reflected in sectors which are highly sensitive to variations in aggregate spending, such as those which produce construction inputs and consumer durables (especially the automotive industry, which was also affected by events in the Brazilian economy). The manufacturing production index for October was significantly lower than it had been 12 months earlier.

Unemployment in the country's major urban areas was down to 13.2% in May 1998 (13.7% in October 1997) and the labour participation rate rose slightly. The following months saw a decline in both employment and the labour supply, and the net result was that the statistics for August showed no significant change in the unemployment rate. Figures for October show a decrease in the unemployment rate (to 12.4%). Data on formal employment in the metropolitan area signal a persistent decline; this has been going on for years in the case of employment covered by traditional open-ended contracts, whereas the number of workers on probationary contracts has increased.

Over the first 11 months of the year, the consumer price index rose by 0.7% (0.2% during the same period in 1997). The increase was mainly due to rising food

prices (2%), particularly for meat, owing to a contraction in the supply of livestock for slaughter. There was significant deflation in wholesale prices (more than 5%) between December 1997 and November 1998.

The current account deficit widened to US$ 5.7 billion during the first half of 1998 compared to US$ 3.65 billion during the same period in 1997. This was mainly attributable to an increase in the merchandise trade deficit caused by rising imports. There was also a worsening deficit under the headings of interest payments, profits and dividends. The non-financial public sector registered a slight increase in capital inflows. Foreign direct investment continued to rise, while the private sector's placement of debt instruments declined slightly. Banking operations once again produced a net capital outflow, although it was smaller in volume than it had been in the first half of 1997.

Taking the year as a whole, the value of merchandise exports is thought to have been similar to the figure for 1997, despite the steep fall (about 9%) in unit values. Figures for the first eight months show a significant increase in the value of exports of manufactured goods, especially motor vehicles, chemicals and iron and steel products. Sales of primary goods also rose despite falling prices, particularly in the case of cereals. Declining prices affected fuel sales as well. Among natural resource-based manufactures, exports of edible oils increased but meat sales were down. Brazil's share in total exports in the first eight months of 1998 (29.4%) was a little lower than the average for the previous year. Towards the end of the year, a decline was observed in sales to the Mercosur area in sectors such as motor vehicles.

During the first eight months of the year imports were considerably higher (10.4%) than during the same period in 1997, with a very sharp increase (21%) in purchases of capital goods. In mid-1998 the demand for imports began to weaken, and growth for the year as a whole is forecast to be around 6%.

BOLIVIA

For the sixth consecutive year, growth in the Bolivian economy was in the 4%-5% range. Following the price adjustments implemented at the end of 1997, inflation continued to decline gradually and was expected to be under 7% by December 1998. The fiscal gap widened to the equivalent of 4% of GDP owing to a combination of increased outlays for the implementation of pension system reforms and lower income due to falling hydrocarbon prices.

The tumbling prices of Bolivia's main export products, owing to the effects of the international crisis, led to a substantial widening of the current account deficit. Imports continued to rise swiftly. The real exchange rate remained stable in relation to the United States dollar, but the local currency appreciated against the currencies of the country's other major trading partners. The current account deficit was in large part financed by the plentiful inflows of foreign investment associated with the construction of the gas pipeline to Brazil and with what is referred to in Bolivia as the "capitalization" (i.e., privatization) of State assets in, among others, the telecommunications sector.

Priority continued to be given to consolidating the macroeconomic stabilization process but, as was expected, the operation of the new pension system made it more difficult to keep public finances in balance. During a prolonged transition period, the pension reforms will entail a decline in State revenue while, at the same time, the pensions being drawn under the previous system will continue to be paid out of public funds. To make up for this extra burden, the authorities have opted for reductions in public-sector investment. The first part of the year saw an upswing in transfers from Yacimientos Petrolíferos Fiscales Bolivianos (YPFB) as a result of the increase in domestic fuel prices announced in December 1997. Nevertheless, those transfers were far from sufficient to make up for the decline in royalties caused by the slump in international crude oil prices.

Monetary policy was, for the most part, contractionary. In the context of a shrinking monetary base, the broad measure of the local-currency money supply (M2) remained stable for the first eight months of the year, while M'2, which includes foreign currency, grew more slowly than during the same period in 1997. Interest rates continued to fall slowly.

Price stability and the preservation of a stable and competitive exchange rate remained the goals of economic policy in 1998. The real exchange rate against the dollar held steady, but the boliviano appreciated against the currencies of several major trading partners, especially Brazil, Chile, Mexico and

BOLIVIA: MAIN ECONOMIC INDICATORS

	1996	1997	1998[a]
	Annual rate of variation		
Gross domestic product	4.4	4.2	4.5
Consumer prices	7.9	6.7	7.8
Real wages	1.1	8.2	[a]
Money (M1)	10.4	15.6	9.0
Real effective exchange rate[b]	-6.6	-2.5	-4.7
Terms of trade	-14.8	3.4	-4.5
	Percentages		
Urban unemployment rate	3.8	4.4	...
Fiscal balance/GDP	-2.0	-3.4	-4.1
Real deposit rate	9.4	7.6	10.2
Real lending rate	43.4	41.0	37.2
	Millions of dollars		
Exports of goods and services	1 313	1 362	1 310
Imports of goods and services	1 731	2 048	2 145
Current account	-404	-714	-805
Capital and financial account	672	807	720
Overall balance	268	93	-85

Source: See the statistical appendix.
[a] Preliminary estimates.
[b] A negative rate signifies an appreciation of the currency in real terms.

some Asian countries. The management of the exchange rate was facilitated by sizeable foreign capital inflows associated with the privatization of public-sector enterprises and other direct investments.

Overall demand grew by a little over 6%; private fixed investment rose by 20%, thereby serving as an important stimulus for the growth of demand. Consumption increased somewhat less than GDP, and physical exports tended to stagnate. As for total supply, output grew by 4.5% and there was a noticeable surge in imports (6.3%).

Thanks to the implementation of development programmes by newly privatized enterprises and numerous foreign investment projects in the farming, mining, electric power and natural gas sectors, FDI continued to be the most dynamic component of private investment. Some of the largest investments in the country are being made in connection with the construction of the gas pipeline to Brazil and the exploration of oilfields and natural gas deposits.

The agricultural sector contracted by about 3.1%. Unfavourable weather conditions caused the farming sector to shrink by 5%, although this was partly offset by a 2% increase in livestock output. The forestry, fishing and hunting sector grew by 4.4%. In the mining industry, the only branches that performed well were gold and silver, but their increased output was enough to allow the sector as a whole to grow by almost 4%. The State-owned mining conglomerate (the Bolivian Mining Corporation, or Comibol) contracted by 12% as a consequence of the drop in zinc and tin production. Medium-scale mining was the only segment to show a significant expansion (9.5%), thanks to notable increases in silver and gold output (18% and 19%, respectively). Output of other ores fell, particularly in the cases of antimony (-32%), tin (-27%) and lead (-21%). Small-scale mining was down by just over 1%, mostly because of decreases in the output of tin (-20%) and lead (-8%). The manufacturing sector grew by 4% as a result of the strong performances of paper and paper products, beverages, non-metallic mineral products, and textiles, wearing apparel and leather. There was

considerable growth in the electricity, gas and water sector (6%), where there was also a significant increase in investments both for the domestic market and for hydroelectric power exports, mainly to Brazil. There was a 24.4% boom in telecommunications thanks to the expansion of national and international telephone services (37% and 26%, respectively); this recently privatized sector has benefited from a generous share of FDI. Construction was up by 21% relative to 1997, largely because of the progress being made in building the gas pipeline to Brazil. Hydrocarbon extraction rose by almost 11% overall as a result of the vigorous increase in the production of crude oil (19%); natural gas output increased by 4%.

During the first 11 months of 1998, the consumer price index showed a cumulative increase of 4.6%, and it appeared quite possible that it might end the year below the 6.5% target figure set for the year. The Government's decision in December 1997 to raise hydrocarbon prices caused strong aftershocks in early 1998, and in the first two months of 1998 alone, the CPI consequently registered a cumulative increase of 2.2%. However, inflation slowed considerably in the second and third quarters.

In the external sector, imports rose and exports fell. The current account deficit increased relative to 1997, exceeding 9% of GDP. The steep drop in the prices of the country's main agro-industrial and mining exports was partly compensated for by increased sales volumes. Imports climbed sharply during most of 1998, with major increases in almost all segments, especially intermediate goods. More than 80% of the country's hefty current account deficit was covered by FDI. International reserves fell to the equivalent of seven months' worth of imports.

The debt relief scheme for heavily-indebted poor countries came into force in 1998, and Bolivia was declared to be eligible for this programme owing to its relatively low level of development and high incidence of poverty, as well as the high ratings which its macroeconomic policies have earned it thanks to the progress being made in the areas of economic stabilization and structural reform. The application of this scheme will bring about a reduction of approximately 20% (US$ 448 million) in the net present value of Bolivia's public external debt. Of that amount, US$ 157 million will be provided by bilateral institutions and the remaining US$ 291 million by multilateral bodies.

BRAZIL

Large fiscal and external deficits made Brazil's economy highly vulnerable to international turbulence in 1998. The severe adjustment measures applied by the Government held back output growth to a mere 0.5%, and per capita GDP consequently fell by 0.8%. The collapse of the Russian economy in August led to a repeat of the damage caused a few months earlier by the Asian crisis, with massive capital flight and the loss of access to international financing, all of which sparked wild fluctuations on Brazil's foreign-exchange market. To keep their promise to maintain the country's existing exchange-rate policy, the authorities once again resorted to spectacular interest rate hikes that drove up annualized real interest rates to over 35%. In the last quarter of 1998 the increasingly steep decline in reserves and the uncertainty reigning in international credit markets forced the Government to adopt a package of measures within the framework of an agreement with the IMF under which US$ 41.5 billion in financial assistance is to be provided by multilateral bodies and a number of industrialized countries.

The Government's **adjustment policies** strengthened the stabilization process to such an extent that the rate of price increases was held down to just 3%, but the figures for economic activity, employment, wages and the external sector were disappointing. According to projections for the year as a whole, industrial output were down by over 2%; unemployment rose to 7.8%, which was more than a third higher than in 1997; and real wages were stagnant. The country's hefty current account deficit shrank slightly, but the performance of the capital account was unfavourable. In the early part of the year international reserves swelled by more than

BRAZIL: GROSS DOMESTIC PRODUCT AND INFLATION
(Percentage variation)

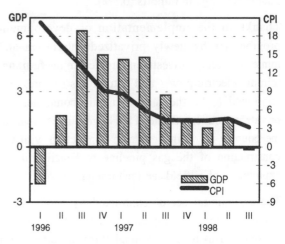

Source: ECLAC, on the basis of official figures.

US$ 20 billion, reaching almost US$ 72 billion by the end of May, but from August onward they eroded swiftly and had fallen to just US$ 42 billion by late November.

The external adjustment had a direct, adverse impact on fiscal accounts. The public-sector deficit is expected to be 7% of GDP (versus 6.1% in 1997), with the increase being largely attributable to the higher cost of servicing the public-sector debt, since outlays for interest payments rose from 5.2% to 7.2% of GDP. This heavier financial load was compounded by factors that hindered the achievement of a better outturn on primary accounts at the various levels of the government structure. There were some improvements at the federal level, but they were not large enough to cover the increased social security deficit, and the total net public debt by the end of the

BRAZIL: MAIN ECONOMIC INDICATORS

	1996	1997	1998[a]
	Annual rate of variation		
Gross domestic product	2.9	3.0	0.5
Consumer prices	9.1	4.3	2.6
Real wages	7.9	2.6	0.3
Money (M1)	4.6	58.9	12.3
Real effective exchange rate[b]	-5.8	-1.1	2.5
Terms of trade	-8.1	5.8	0.0
	Percentages		
Urban unemployment rate	5.4	5.7	7.8
Fiscal balance/GDP	-5.9	-6.2	-7.0
Real deposit rate	16.5	19.6	22.8
Real lending rate	41.6	44.1	85.8
	Millions of dollars		
Exports of goods and services	54 524	60 252	60 000
Imports of goods and services	69 110	79 821	76 750
Current account	-24 347	-33 484	-32 450
Capital and financial account	33 121	25 647	17 450
Overall balance	8 774	-7 837	-15 000

Source: See the statistical appendix.
[a] Preliminary estimates.
[b] A negative rate signifies an appreciation of the currency in real terms.

year is therefore expected to amount to 42% of GDP (as opposed to 34% at the end of 1997).

Economic policy pursued three immediate objectives in succession during the course of 1998: from January to April, the implementation of monetary and fiscal measures designed to stave off the effects of the Asian crisis; from May to August, the introduction of economic stimuli in order to bring about a recovery in the level of activity; and from September onward, the application of mechanisms to cope with the impact of the Russian crisis and the design of an external assistance and fiscal policy package to prevent the collapse of the Brazilian economy despite worldwide expectations to the contrary.

During the first of these periods, following the resumption of external capital flows, the central bank paved the way for a slow descent of interest rates. International reserves began to build up again in February, peaking at US$ 73.8 billion in May. The overnight interest rate, which had approached 3% per month in late 1997, fell to 1.63% in May.

In order to bolster its accounts, the Government implemented new rules on the taxation of income from financial assets, lowered the spending limits laid down in the 1998 budget, and intensified its efforts to curb borrowing by state and municipal governments.

When the impact of restrictive measures on economic activity became clear during the period from May to August, as industrial output slumped and unemployment rates reached unprecedented levels, the tax on financial operations was reduced from 15% to less than 6% and the motor vehicle production tax was cut by five percentage points; in addition, some budgetary limits were reintroduced. With the stabilization of capital flows and international reserves, the central bank continued to reduce interest rates, although more slowly than before. This set of measures paved the way for a recovery in the level of activity.

In August there was another episode of **massive capital flight.** International reserves fell by US$ 24 billion as a result of the exodus of short-term funds and the decrease in bond rollovers. The Central Bank once again raised its top interest rate, this time to 49% per annum. To strengthen the credibility of its commitment to fiscal equilibrium, the central government made its targets for the primary balance legally binding and cut budgetary ceilings by 20%.

In October, the persistence of capital flight forced the authorities to implement a **more drastic fiscal adjustment**, sign an agreement with the International Monetary Fund and seek help from industrialized countries in re-establishing lines of credit. In late October the Government submitted a fiscal package to Congress whose aim was to boost the primary balance by almost 26 billion reais. The package provided for increases in the tax rate on financial transactions (from 0.2% to 0.38%), in social security contributions (from 2% to 3%), as well as requiring that they also be paid by the previously exempt financial sector, and in the social security taxes to be paid by civil servants, including retired federal government officials. In addition, a further cut of 8.9 billion reais was made in the proposed budget for 1999.

The constitutional reforms relating to government service adopted during the latter part of the second quarter and the social security reforms passed in November will produce no immediate fiscal savings, but they will make the management of State finances more flexible and therefore appear to be in keeping with the measures set out in the adjustment package.

In July, control of the State telephone system, Telebrás, was transferred to private ownership for approximately US$ 19 billion in what was the largest privatization operation ever to be carried out in Latin America. The sale of assets or concessions in the port and electricity sectors also continued. In addition, state governments moved forward with their own privatization programmes (energy distribution, banking, railways, and urban train services).

The **level of activity** was hurt by high interest rates, and the timid economic expansion that had appeared to be starting up in the second quarter was halted by the Russian crisis. The manufacturing sector was hit the hardest by monetary measures, and consumer goods industries contracted, particularly in the case of consumer durables. The agricultural sector shrank 0.5% because of losses in rice, corn and bean harvests. Rising interest rates also cut growth in construction to 3.4% in the third quarter of 1998, compared to 8.5% the year before.

The sluggishness of the economy's production sectors and the cooling of demand relieved inflationary pressures, and **the CPI** consequently rose by just 3%. The trend towards smaller increases or even decreases in prices for services and non-tradable goods strengthened, providing further proof of the flexibility

of relative prices since the introduction of the *Real* Plan. Indeed, in cities such as São Paulo where the impact of restrictive measures is strongest, there seems to have been some deflation.

Between January and October, industrial employment fell by 7.1% in São Paulo and by 4.6% nationwide. There were also considerable job losses in the commercial sector. As a result, the **unemployment rate** rose to nearly 8% (as compared to 5.8% in 1997).

To avoid any further deterioration of the situation in the labour market, a system of "temporary resignation" was set up as a way of reducing severance payments; regulations governing part-time and temporary work contracts were established; flexible working hours were introduced in order to lower overtime costs; unemployment benefits for more experienced workers were increased; and improvements were made in the training and retraining systems.

During the period from January to September, the average incomes of employed persons showed no increase over the corresponding period of 1997. However, a comparison of the figures for September 1998 and September 1997 reveals the first decrease in the index of average wages to be recorded in the past five years.

The **external sector** exhibited some degree of vulnerability owing to the size of the current account deficit; this problem has been heightened by the substantial deterioration seen in the real exchange rate since the introduction of the *Real* Plan in June 1994. The policy of controlled devaluations (that amounted to a nominal rate of 7.5% in 1998) has been one of the mainstays of economic policy. However, this overvaluation was reduced by 3% thanks to very low inflation and the weakening of the United States dollar against several world currencies.

As of the end of the third quarter, manufacturing **exports** were up 6.6%, in contrast with commodities (down 12%) and semi-manufactured products (down 1.5%), suggesting that total external sales for the year will turn out to have fallen by around 0.6%, a far cry from the targeted 11% increase. The shortfall can be attributed to the external crisis and to supply-side constraints in the Brazilian economy. Lower international prices and insufficient growth in the number of shipments led to a substantial decline in earnings from major agricultural exports, such as coffee and soybeans, and from aluminium-, iron- and steel-based semi-manufactures. Exports of manufactures were boosted by the upswing in sales of products having a relatively higher technological content, including motor vehicles and aircraft. Exports to Asia, including Japan, fell by 28% (49% in the five countries more seriously affected by the Asian crisis) and, while these markets represent a modest percentage of the country's total sales, this nonetheless affected the performance of the external sector as a whole.

The one-third drop in the merchandise trade deficit was mostly due to the 4.8% reduction in the value of imports. Factors of particular importance in this respect included the lower value of fuel purchases, thanks to the downturn in international oil prices, and of imports of durable goods, owing to weaker domestic demand. Motor vehicle imports were the exception, increasing by 7.4% to US$ 2 billion.

Foreign capital inflows plunged in the third quarter. Despite a balance of payments surplus of US$ 18.7 billion at the end of the second quarter, by the end of September Brazil was running a cumulative deficit for the year of US$ 6.5 billion. Net outflows in the form of payments for factor services were US$ 2.7 billion higher than in 1997, with a 22% rise in profit remittances. The capital account showed net outflows of US$ 5.9 billion in the third quarter, and cumulative net inflows for the year were therefore down to US$ 16.9 billion. Direct investments continued to rise, reaching US$ 22 billion in October. More than 25% of those inflows were for privatizations, which was 51% more than in the same period of 1997.

CHILE

Chile's balance of payments was hit hard by the external crisis. As a result, growth and spending were held down in an economy which had enjoyed almost 15 years of rapid expansion. The combination of internal adjustment and the impact of the external crisis led to a growth rate of only about 4% (7.1% in 1997) and pushed the current account deficit up to 7% of GDP. Inflation was down again, to about 4.5%, within the target set by the Central Bank. Although the steep drop in international copper prices has reduced the income of the public sector, the latter will once again end the year with a surplus.

With the deterioration of the terms of trade, high interest rates, and the upward trend of the exchange rate, **private spending has been reined in severely**. Very high interest rates over several months kept spending down and helped to narrow the external deficit, but they also slowed investment and

CHILE: GROSS DOMESTIC PRODUCT AND INFLATION

(Percentage variation)

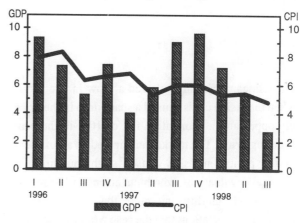

Source: ECLAC, on the basis of official figures.

productive activity, resulting in an anticipated fall in the level of output for the fourth quarter.

CHILE: MAIN ECONOMIC INDICATORS

	1996	1997	1998[a]
	Annual rate of variation		
Gross domestic product	7.0	7.1	4.0
Consumer prices	6.6	6.0	4.3
Real wages	4.1	2.4	2.8
Money (M1)	-7.8	20.0	-5.3
Real effective exchange rate [b]	-3.6	-6.7	2.2
Terms of trade	-16.6	3.8	-10.5
	Percentages		
Unemployment rate	6.4	6.1	6.1
Fiscal balance/GDP	2.3	1.9	0.7
Real deposit rate	6.4	5.8	10.1
Real lending rate	10.1	9.2	15.1
	Millions of dollars		
Exports of goods and services	18 771	20 608	18 940
Imports of goods and services	20 219	22 219	22 445
Current account	-3 744	-4 058	-5 160
Capital and financial account	6 249	7 243	2 460
Overall balance	2 505	3 185	-2 700

Source: See the statistical appendix.
[a] Preliminary estimates.
[b] A negative rate signifies an appreciation of the currency in real terms.

The Chilean economy suffered a blow in late 1997, when the Asian crisis caused a sharp drop in the price of copper and a cumulative fall of 10% in the **real exchange rate.** The market anticipated an adjustment of the parity, and this caused slight but unusual nominal devaluations, which put an end to 10 months of nominal stability and more than five years of persistent expectations that the peso would appreciate. High levels of activity and spending in the last quarter of 1997 (9.6% and 13.7%) and the escalation of the current account deficit caused nervousness in the financial system, bringing about a drastic portfolio adjustment with a shift towards dollar-denominated assets and liabilities, a process which continued until mid-1998.

In January, in the absence of nominal anchors, exchange and interest rate volatility intensified. The exchange rate climbed to 453 pesos to the dollar (414 in October 1997), while the interbank rate soared, coming close to 100% in real terms. The Central Bank decided to raise the real interbank rate from 6.5% to 7%, a measure which the market viewed as insufficient. Only after a further increase to 8.5% was the credibility of macroeconomic management restored.

In June the pressure on the peso resumed, this time in anticipation of possible repercussions for copper prices and external financing from the yen's fall against the dollar. In four weeks, **international reserves** fell by US$ 1.3 billion.

The Central Bank cut the reserve requirement on external credits from 30% to 10%, seeking to reduce the cost of external financing; introduced dollar-indexed paper; and, lastly, narrowed the currency band from 12.5% on either side of the reference parity to a floor of 3.5% below the "dollar acuerdo" reference exchange rate and a ceiling of only 2% above it. This improved confidence in exchange rate stability and the achievement of the inflation rate target.

In September the collapse of the Russian economy and the impending crisis in Brazil set off another attack on the peso. The Central Bank managed to fend it off with a package of measures including: (i) raising the ceiling of the currency band from 2% to 3.5% and gradual widening of the band; (ii) eliminating the 2.4% discount for external inflation in the calculation of the price of the dollar; and (iii) linking the flotation of the dollar to expected, rather than past inflation. This provided some room for the exchange rate to rise. In addition, the rate used for controlling the money supply was raised from 8.5% to 14% and the reserve requirement for external capital inflows was reduced to zero. A change for the better on the international scene in the last quarter helped to improve the outlook, allowing for orderly devaluation and gradual relaxation of monetary policy. The interest rate fell from the level of 14.5% to which it had risen in mid-September to 12% in mid-October, 10% in early November and 8.5% in late November.

Fiscal policy helped to contain spending through a 5.5% cut in planned outlays for 1998. Despite declining revenue from taxation and from copper, the public sector will once again show a surplus, which this year will be equivalent to 0.7% of GDP.

Thanks to improved stability on the external scene, calm returned to Chile's foreign exchange and money markets during the fourth quarter. The **stock market** registered strong gains, following cumulative losses for the year of about 25%, while there was a considerable adjustment in spending and inflation continued to fall.

As for **legislation**, the establishment of an international offshore stock exchange in Chile was approved. An infrastructure fund was created in order to improve the stability and continuity time of financial flows and commitments in relation to public works carried out under concession. A tariff reduction was approved whereby the general tariff of 11% on imports will be reduced to 6% within five years. Incentives were created for private savings in the form of shares, financial deposits and dividends from shares in limited corporations.

In late September the economy showed annualized **growth** of 5.4%, with increases which had declined from 7.9% in the first quarter to 2.7% in the fourth. Growth in expenditure had slowed even more markedly, the corresponding rates of increase being 15.6% and 0.5% for the same two quarters. The growth differential between expenditure and output, which had reached 7.7 percentage points during the first quarter, turned negative in the third quarter. Economic growth for the year as a whole is expected to be around 4%, with a slowdown in the pace of both output and expenditure in the fourth quarter.

The 12-month **inflation** rate was down to 4.3% in November, slightly below the 4.5% target. This favourable trend was due to a considerable slowing in tradables prices, particularly during the fourth quarter, helped by lower international inflation and exchange rate stability.

Growth in employment was declining, reacting with the usual time-lag to changes in the level of activity. Annualized growth in employment was 2.5% in the second quarter and 1.3% in the third, with an average of 1.9% for the first nine months. The unemployment rate, which stood at 5.3% in January, was approaching 7% at the end of the year, although, with slower growth in the labour force, the increases were marginal compared to the same period in 1997.

There was also slower growth in nominal **wage levels**, although they continued to benefit from previously high levels of activity. In late October the average annual variation in nominal wages stood at 7.9% and that in real wages at 2.5%.

The **current account** deficit will amount to about US$ 5.2 billion, equivalent to 7% of GDP, and the capital account should show a surplus of US$ 2.46 billion, less than half the surplus in 1997. International reserves are expected to show a loss of US$ 2.7 billion. The unfavourable current account result is basically due to the trade deficit of US$ 3.5 billion, which can be attributed to a deterioration in the terms of trade of close to 10%. Exports are expected to be down 11% and imports unchanged.

COLOMBIA

The economic recovery begun in 1997 remained strong up through the first quarter of 1998 but then started to falter in the second quarter; the net result was that growth for the year was about 2%. The shocks associated with the Asian and Russian crises reduced the availability of foreign capital and drove down export earnings by triggering steep drops in oil, coffee and coal prices. Prolonged turbulence on the foreign-exchange front began in the first half of the year, depriving economic authorities of much of their manoeuvring room and pushing up interest rates. These high rates cooled off production activity, weakened the financial system and, by increasing the public sector's interest burden, widened the central government's fiscal deficit to the equivalent of 4.8% of GDP. The balance-of-payments current account deficit also worsened, reaching 6.6% of output. Despite some upturn in employment, the situation in the labour market deteriorated to such an extent that the urban unemployment rate exceeded 15%. Some of these adverse economic effects may have been aggravated by the erosion of public order and the still uncertain outlook for the peace negotiations.

Despite these problems, the softening of monetary policy in recent months in response to more stable monetary conditions led to greater optimism at the end of the year. The central bank's inflation target was met for the second consecutive year, and the real exchange rate reached a level that will have a positive influence on the balance of payments. In addition, the new Government announced it would take steps to strengthen the fiscal adjustment measures introduced during the final years of the previous Administration.

Defending the local currency came to be a very important task in early 1998 and soon became the prime objective of **economic policy**. Pressure on the exchange-rate band had already been apparent in the last quarter of 1997. The harmful effects of the Asian crisis added to the deficits on the fiscal account and

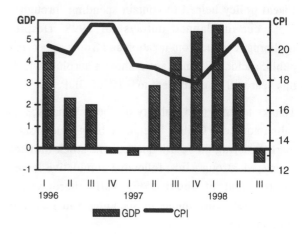

COLOMBIA: GROSS DOMESTIC PRODUCT AND INFLATION
(Percentage variation)

Source: ECLAC, on the basis of official figures.

the balance-of-payments current account. It also became clear that the abundant supply of foreign exchange that had been expected to result from the oil boom was not going to materialize any time soon. Economic actors therefore modified their expectations and began to anticipate a further depreciation of the local currency.

The authorities chose to defend the existing exchange-rate band, which had a gradient of 13% and a width of 15 percentage points. Initially, the central bank facilitated private access to external financing, increased the cost of liquidity, and sold foreign exchange. In May, however, the intensity of the run on the currency forced the Banco de la República to limit the amount of funds used to replenish liquidity, and the interbank interest rate skyrocketed, climbing as high as 80% at one point. This increase quickly spread throughout the interest-rate structure. Turbulence on world markets in August renewed the pressure on the foreign-exchange market. On 2 September, the central bank decided to raise the level of the band by nine percentage points, while leaving its gradient and width

COLOMBIA: MAIN ECONOMIC INDICATORS

	1996	1997	1998[a]
	Annual rate of variation		
Gross domestic product	21	30	20
Consumer prices	216	177	163
Real wages	15	28	-07
Money (M1)	164	215	-02
Real effective exchange rate [b]	-73	-64	36
Terms of trade	38	117	-62
	Percentages		
Urban unemployment rate	112	124	151
Fiscal balance/GDP	-20	-36	-34
Real deposit rate	77	52	93
Real lending rate	172	142	179
	Millions of dollars		
Exports of goods and services	14 590	15 888	15 765
Imports of goods and services	16 746	18 756	19 135
Current account	-4 946	-5 683	-6 060
Capital and financial account	6 428	5 653	4 635
Overall balance	1 482	- 30	-1 425

Source: See the statiscal appendix.

[a] Preliminary estimates.

[b] A negative rate signifies an appreciation of the currency in real terms.

unchanged. Various events in late October helped to improve the outlook. Multilateral agencies agreed to lend over US$ 2 billion to Colombia in 1999 and a similar amount in 2000, which will help to finance the external deficit. Renewed confidence on world markets also opened up the possibility of obtaining new private credits. In October the Government began issuing dollar-denominated bonds on the domestic market, helping to alleviate the pressure on the exchange-rate band. The nominal depreciation of the peso is expected to amount to about 20% by the end of the year.

Monetary management became more restrictive, and monetary aggregates therefore grew less than had been expected. The money supply increased by barely 1%

up to October, while broad money rose by a below-inflation rate of 16%, causing a rapid slowdown in credit growth. Consequently, the average deposit rate in the financial system rose from 24% in January to 36% in June and remained close to that level during the third and fourth quarters. Lending rates also rose during the first half of the year, from 33% to 45%, reaching the highest levels in real terms registered since the beginning of the decade. In order to counter a moderate deterioration in the financial system, the Government introduced extraordinary measures following its declaration of an "economic emergency" on 16 November and levied a tax on financial transactions that was designed to bring in 2.5 billion pesos (the equivalent of 2% of GDP) to strengthen the Financial Institutions Guarantee Fund (FOGAFIN). It also took steps to help low-income mortgage holders and participants in the cooperative savings and housing system.

Relatively calm conditions in the foreign-exchange market in the latter part of the year enabled the central bank to inject more liquidity into the financial system, to lower reserve requirements and begin to pay interest on those reserves, and to lower interest rates for cash replenishment.

Fiscal balances were negative, with the central government deficit rising to 4.8% of GDP. Total income fell by 5% in real terms, while total expenditure increased slightly (1.4%), since the deep cut in investment (-37%) was not sufficient to cover the increased debt burden (30%) resulting from higher interest rates. In fact, total central government spending on items other than interest payments fell in real terms in 1998. Since the other public agencies were able to balance their accounts, the surplus in the social security system had the effect of reducing the consolidated non-financial public sector's deficit to 3.4% of GDP. The central bank's quasi-fiscal surplus of close to 1% of GDP also eased the fiscal situation. When the new Government took office in August, it announced measures to correct fiscal imbalances and submitted a tax reform bill to Congress which is expected to pass in the near future.

Economic activity lost the momentum it had gained from the previous year's upswing, which was reflected in GDP growth of 5.7% in the first quarter of 1998. GDP growth had turned negative by the third quarter (-0.6%), however, and the figure for the year as a whole is therefore estimated at around 2%. As far as individual sectors are concerned, mining and quarrying was the only outstanding performer, with a growth rate close to 20% (in large part thanks to the results posted by the petroleum industry). Construction, on the other hand, was unable to pull itself out of the recession that overtook it three years ago.

The upturn in **employment** was not strong enough to offset the increase in the labour force participation rate. Consequently, the urban unemployment rate for Colombia's seven major metropolitan areas exceeded 15%. In view of this situation, job creation has become one of the new Government's top priorities.

The downward trend in **inflation** of recent years was interrupted in the first half of 1998, when, in annualized terms, the cumulative increase in the CPI for the period was over 20%. The damage sustained by the agricultural sector as a consequence of El Niño accounts for a large part of that inflationary surge. In the second half of the year, however, favourable weather conditions and the effects of the Government's tight monetary policy helped to cut back the rate of price increases substantially. Accordingly, the inflation rate is expected to stand at about 16% for the year as a whole.

Total **exports** for the first eight months of the year were down 3.7%, whereas imports were up 7.3%. As a result, the year is expected to close with a current account deficit of more than US$ 6 billion, or 6.6% of GDP.

An increase in the volume of the country's main commodity exports (petroleum, coffee and coal) did not make up for the decline in their international prices, and export earnings from these items are therefore expected to be lower. On the other hand, non-traditional exports were up 4.3% as of August. Imports rose considerably (12.3%) during the first two quarters, reflecting the delayed effects of the recovery in economic activity and perhaps expectations of a devaluation as well. However, the growth of imports slowed during the second half of the year as domestic demand slackened, chiefly as a consequence of the stagnation of both private and public investment. **Capital inflows** registered on the financial account fell to US$ 4.64 billion (compared to US$ 5.65 billion the previous year), as a result of which international reserves declined by about US$ 1.4 billion.

ECUADOR

In 1998 the economy of Ecuador suffered from the impact of the El Niño phenomenon, falling petroleum prices, the political uncertainty of an election year and, in the second half of the year, external financing problems resulting from the international crisis. Output grew by a meagre 1%, the financial public sector showed a deficit of 5% of GDP, and the balance-of-payments current account deficit exceeded 9% of GDP. At the same time, inflation rose to 45%.

The disastrous effects of El Niño devastated the country's infrastructure and agricultural sector, and indirectly damaged other activities. Low petroleum prices led to a large fiscal deficit. The impact of the international economic crisis seemed relatively limited to begin with, owing to the embryonic nature of the domestic capital market and the weakness of trade links with the worst affected countries. In the second half of the year, however, the decline in external financing led to liquidity problems and caused turbulence on the foreign exchange market.

Fiscal policy was faced with a considerable contraction in revenue owing to falling petroleum prices, while current expenditure increased substantially. In September, the new Government abolished subsidies on gas, reduced those on electric power and increased the tax on diesel fuel, while awarding poor households a compensatory bonus. It also announced that it would cut public expenditure by the equivalent of 1.3% of GDP. These measures were intended to reduce the public-sector deficit to around 6% of GDP.

The **currency band** system was maintained in order to restrain inflationary expectations and the rate of price increases. On two occasions, however, it became necessary to raise the level of the band, by 7.5% in March and 15% in September, because of the uncertainty reigning in the foreign exchange market and growing inflationary pressures. Nonetheless, on average over the first nine months of 1998 the sucre

ECUADOR: GROSS DOMESTIC PRODUCT AND INFLATION

(Percentage variation)

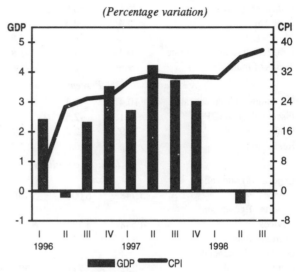

Source: ECLAC, on the basis of official figures.

appreciated by 4%. From September onwards, the scarcity of dollars resulting from the curtailment of external financing led to considerable volatility in the nominal exchange rate and sharp real depreciation of the sucre.

The loss of international reserves resulting from the external imbalance and, at times, from the defence of the exchange rate slowed the growth of liquidity and counteracted the effects of the large fiscal deficit. Beginning in September the Central Bank provided lines of credit to a number of banks while simultaneously intensifying the use of stabilization bonds to limit the expansionary effects of such transactions. As a result, by November growth in the **monetary base** had moderated to 17%, signifying a marked reduction in real terms. The shortage of liquidity led to interest rate rises: the reference lending rate increased to almost 80%, reaching a peak of 14% in real terms in August and then declining gradually.

The **growth** target for 1998 was set at 4%, but late in the year it was estimated that only about 1% growth

ECUADOR: MAIN ECONOMIC INDICATORS

	1996	1997	1998[a]
	Annual rate of variation		
Gross domestic product	2.3	3.3	1.0
Consumer prices	25.6	30.6	45.0
Real wages	5.4	-2.3	...
Money (M1)	35.4	29.7	15.8
Real effective exchange rate [b]	0.4	-4.2	-3.8
Terms of trade	9.6	2.1	-8.4
	Percentages		
Urban unemployment rate	10.4	9.3	...
Fiscal balance/GDP	-3.1	-2.5	-6.0
Real deposit rate	12.9	-2.0	-4.2
Real lending rate	...	10.0	2.5
	Millions of dollars		
Exports of goods and services	5 748	6 000	5 240
Imports of goods and services	4 548	5 787	6 325
Current account	111	- 746	-1 765
Capital and financial account	- 252	779	725
Overall balance	- 141	33	-1 040

Source: See the statistical appendix.
[a] Preliminary estimates.
[b] A negative rate signifies an appreciation of the currency in real terms.

would be achieved, representing a decline of approximately 1% in per capita output.

The El Niño phenomenon caused losses of almost US$ 3 billion and reduced the growth of GDP by 1.3 percentage points. The full brunt of the disaster was borne by agriculture in the coastal area, particularly banana plantations. Tourism also contracted owing to the bad weather. Damage to the transport system indirectly affected various activities, including manufacturing and commerce. Other factors which slowed growth were high interest rates and the deterioration in the terms of trade.

As a result, the economy showed only minimal growth of 0.4% for the first three quarters of the year. Agriculture, petroleum, and financial services contracted, in some cases substantially. Apart from

construction and government services, which should show some expansion as a result of the work of reconstruction, the performance of the country's major activities for the year as a whole was expected to be poorer than in 1997.

The **banking system** suffered from the impact of El Niño on the productive sector and the interruption of external capital inflows. The size of the overdue portfolio expanded considerably, and the authorities had to intervene in a number of country's major banks, while some banks received liquidity loans from the Central Bank and others merged to strengthen their competitive position.

The volume of exports, which for several years had been a driving force in the growth of Ecuador's economy, stagnated because of the fall in external demand and the destruction caused by El Niño. Household consumption, the main component of overall demand, only increased at a rate close to that of population growth, since the erosion of real wages and weak job creation prevented stronger recovery in purchasing power. Real minimum **wages** fell for the second consecutive year, this time by about 7%. Gross fixed capital formation expanded a little less than in 1997; this was due to lower growth in private investment, as well as the increased weight of public investment caused by the need to repair the devastation caused by El Niño.

There were two surges in **inflation.** The first took place early in the year, owing to the impact of the disastrous weather on agricultural output and transport; and the second, beginning in September, was caused by the elimination of certain subsidies. As a result, the annualized inflation rate rose to 45% in November.

Exports, which suffered the impact of the aforementioned critical factors, contracted by 20%. There was a 40% drop in the value of petroleum exports, chiefly because of falling prices. The devastation caused by El Niño and the abrupt fall in demand in Asia and Russia weakened banana sales. There was also a small decline in the value of shrimp exports owing to falling prices. In contrast, there was growth in all categories of imports. The **balance of trade,** typically a surplus, went into deficit and caused the current account deficit to approach 10% of GDP.

During the third quarter, international monetary reserves suffered heavy losses owing to growing difficulties in covering the current account deficit, but the situation stabilized in November. Taking the year as a whole, the main source of financing was credit

from multilateral organizations for the reconstruction of infrastructure damaged by El Niño and the stabilization of the balance of payments (Latin American Reserve Fund). In addition, the loss of reserve assets was held down by increased foreign direct investment (US$ 750 million) owing to greater investments in petroleum and the accumulation of delays in servicing the external debt (Paris Club).

PARAGUAY

The Paraguayan economy remained stagnant in 1998 owing to the bad weather that hit the country's important agricultural sector. Uncertainty due to the foreign exchange and financial crisis prompted economic agents to take refuge in the dollar, and by the end of the third quarter the guaraní showed an annualized depreciation of 10% in real terms. By late September, feverish demand for foreign exchange had brought down international reserves to the equivalent of two months of imports. The depreciation of the national currency and the decline in supply of agricultural products brought about an inflationary surge. By late November the annualized variation in the consumer price index reached 16%, ten points higher than a year earlier and the highest level in four years.

The main goal of **economic policy** was to contain inflationary pressures, so that tight monetary and fiscal policies were implemented. These, however, were eroded by the prolonged banking crisis.

Central government accounts will end the year with a deficit of 1.5% of GDP, somewhat higher than in 1997, owing to the virtual stagnation of revenue accompanied by increased spending. Revenue was undercut by the slower pace of economic activity; efforts to reduce tax evasion did not succeed in making up for the loss. Current revenue contracted because of declining receipts from value added tax, import duties and income taxes. This decline resulted from the

PARAGUAY: MAIN ECONOMIC INDICATORS

	1996	1997	1998[a]
	Annual rate of variation		
Gross domestic product	1.1	2.6	0.0
Consumer prices	8.2	6.2	16.0
Real wages	3.1	-0.4	-0.8
Money (M1)	2.1	13.9	4.3
Real effective exchange rate[b]	-4.3	-1.7	10.9
Terms of trade	10.5	20.8	-4.8
	Percentages		
Urban unemployment rate	8.2	7.1	...
Fiscal balance/GDP [c]	-0.8	-0.2	-1.5
Real deposit rate	9.8	9.8	-13.8
Real lending rate	22.2	20.7	-4.8
	Millions of dollars		
Exports of goods and services	4 547	4 184	3 895
Imports of goods and services	5 022	4 960	4 280
Current account	-317	-642	-235
Capital and financial account	289	444	105
Overall balance	-28	-198	-130

Source: See the statistical appendix.
[a] Preliminary estimates.
[b] A negative rate signifies an appreciation of the currency in real terms.
[c] Beginning 1998, calculated on an accrual basis.

disappointing performance of economic activity and from lower levels of imports owing to the depreciation of the currency. Royalties from the Itaipú and Yacyretá binational hydroelectric dams increased by almost 50%, but were insufficient to make up for the loss of revenue from other sources.

Despite the implementation of austerity measures, overall expenditure expanded because of larger outlays on wages and salaries, interest payments and social security benefits. Physical investment projects were also expected to increase during the fourth quarter. Net lending by the Central Bank to the public sector should therefore be about 40% higher than in 1997. From 1998 onwards, the Ministry of Finance will present the results of fiscal management on an accrual, rather than a cash basis.

Monetary policy encountered many problems in its efforts to control inflationary pressure. The critical situation in the banking sector, the poor outlook for the productive sector and fear of a traumatic devaluation of the Brazilian *real* caused uncertainty among economic agents, which led to a run on the guaraní. The Central Bank intervened to defend the currency during the first and third quarters, which cost it US$ 140 million over the year, almost one-fifth of its total dollar reserves. To boost demand for guaraníes, it floated monetary regulation instruments with an average yield of about 25%, more than 13 points higher than the average for 1997. This was another factor in the upward movement of interest rates. By September, however, the national currency showed an annualized depreciation of 10% in real terms. This caused further damage to fiscal accounts by swelling the external debt expressed in national currency.

The Central Bank continued with its financial system reform policy for the fourth successive year. During the first quarter the liquidation of two of the country's largest financial institutions was announced, and during the third quarter the Central Bank had to intervene in two banks and another financial institution. The liquidation of one of the banks was scheduled for late November.

At the end of the third quarter, despite open market operations and sales of foreign currencies, the annualized variation in money in circulation stood at 12%. Reactions to the banking crisis led to the substitution of money in circulation for demand and savings deposits. As a result, the M1 money supply grew slightly (3%), while M2 contracted. A clear preference for deposits in dollars was also observed; as of September, these showed an annualized increase of 48%.

Adverse weather conditions damaged **agricultural productivity**, and the sector's slight growth was basically due to an increase in area sown. This was particularly true in the case of the cotton crop, which recovered after a drop of more than 50% the previous year, although it remained well below the average for the decade. Yield was down, owing to excessive amounts of rainfall and problems with plant health. These difficulties were compounded by the crisis in the financial system, which made access to credit difficult for producers. On the other hand, the soybean crop once again topped the previous year's record, although not by as much. As in the case of cotton, this performance was due to increased area sown rather than improved yields. Activity in agriculture, forestry, construction, industry and commerce declined.

The cumulative variation of the **consumer price index** as of November was 15%, so that the inflation figure should be about 16% by the end of the year, ten percentage points higher than the 1997 figure. This change was mostly due to rising food prices caused by the shorter supply of agricultural products and the sharp depreciation of the guaraní. The cost of education, health and transport services also rose.

The **minimum wage** increased by 9% in nominal terms, but with annualized inflation of 16% this meant a substantial decline in real terms. However, the real average wage of manual workers showed an average increase for the year of 4%, owing to pay rises in the basic services and construction sectors.

The **current account** remained in deficit, but significantly less so than in 1997: the gap narrowed from US$ 640 million to US$ 240 million. One of its components, the trade deficit, remained sizeable, although about a third of imports and almost two thirds of exports consist of unregistered transactions. **Capital flows** diminished to 25% of their 1997 level, amounting to a little more than US$ 100 million.

The value of **registered exports** during the first nine months of 1998 was down by 12% compared to the same period in 1997. This fall was due to lower cotton

and soybean sales. Both decreased by 13% owing to falling international prices and a decline of almost 30% in demand in Brazil; increased purchases by Argentina were not sufficient to make up the difference. The value of **registered imports** as of September was down by 27% owing to the depreciation of the guaraní, the sluggish performance of the national economy and declining cross-border trade.

PERU

The growth rate of the Peruvian economy fell back to 1% in 1998, as a result of the devastating effect of the El Niño climatic phenomenon and a succession of shocks originating abroad. Rainfall over extensive areas of the country, without precedent in decades, caused the collapse of much of the highway infrastructure and a contraction in the supply of agricultural and fishing products, categories that account for a high percentage of total exports. In addition, the Asian crisis eroded the international price of mining products –especially copper– which are crucial to the Peruvian export basket. Lastly, in September the effects of the international financial crisis set off by the Russian moratorium began to be felt, and tightened the availability of foreign credit to emerging economies.

In the face of severe constraints on the supply side, the Government opted to preserve price stability and concentrated its efforts on reining in demand. It is estimated that by year's end the 12-month accumulated inflation rate will be below 6%.

Fiscal policy played a restraining role and brought about reductions of 3% in public consumption and 4% in capital expenditure. The spending cuts offset the decrease in revenues caused by the economic slowdown and a reduction in the National Housing Fund (FONAVI) tax rate from 7% to 5%. Central government operations produced a deficit equivalent to 0.3% of GDP, while outlays for interest payments

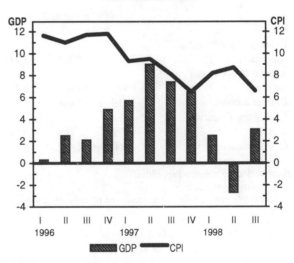

PERU: GROSS DOMESTIC PRODUCT AND INFLATION

Source: ECLAC, on the basis of official figures.

on the external debt amounted to 1.8% of output. The non-financial public sector, as a whole, achieved a current surplus equivalent to 3.8% of GDP, which helped it to finance investment amounting to 4% of GDP, and still end up with a deficit of only 0.1% of output. Privatization proceeds declined again in 1998, this time to half a per cent of GDP, and came largely from the national private sector.

Monetary policy closely tracked the slowdown in the pace of activity and the trend in inflation. The loss of

PERU: MAIN ECONOMIC INDICATORS

	1996	1997	1998[a]
	Annual rate of variation		
Gross domestic product	2.3	7.4	1.0
Consumer prices	11.8	6.5	6.0
Real wages	-4.7	-0.7	-1.6
Money (M1)	18.1	19.3	-6.6
Real effective exchange rate[b]	-1.4	0.6	-0.4
Terms of trade	-3.5	17.0	-8.8
	Percentages		
Urban unemployment rate	8.0	9.2	9.0
Fiscal balance/GDP	-1.0	0.0	-0.1
Real deposit rate	-1.4	3.6	2.7
Real lending rate	17.6	23.0	22.2
	Millions of dollars		
Exports of goods and services	7 312	8 354	7 415
Imports of goods and services	9 985	10 840	10 690
Current account	-3 619	-3 408	-4 120
Capital and financial account	4 579	5 865	3 045
Overall balance	960	2 457	-1 075

Source: See the statistical appendix.

[a] Preliminary estimates.

[b] A negative rate signifies an appreciation of the currency in real terms.

international reserves, which gathered pace from September onward, was compensated for by an expansion in domestic sources of money creation, so that the monetary base grew by 11% over 12 months. However, this increase was not enough to prevent a 6.6% contraction in the money supply (M1), although quasi-money in national currency posted an expansion of 7%. The 16% increase in foreign currency deposits enabled the total liquidity of the system to increase by 11%.

Although Peru has a policy of free capital movement, until June it applied a marginal reserve requirement of 45%, reduced to 35% from July onward in an attempt to encourage foreign capital to remain in the country and thus alleviate the illiquidity of the financial system. The average reserve requirement was also lowered by 1.5% in October and by a similar amount in November, thereby freeing up US$ 280 million, which flowed to banks whose credit lines abroad had not been renewed. The illiquidity of the financial system led to a sharp rise in the interbank interest rate, which in September climbed to 35% but dropped back in subsequent months to between 10% and 12%.

The **productive sectors** hardest hit by the Asian crisis included fishing, where output plummeted to less than half that of a normal year. Sharp reverses were also seen in the agricultural sector and in industrial raw material processing activities. In contrast, the construction and basic services sector showed considerable vigour.

The components underpinning expenditure growth were gross fixed capital formation and exports, whose dynamism was concentrated in the second half of the year. The investment ratio rose to 25%, nearly one percentage point higher than in 1997, and this was financed almost three to one by domestic saving.

The slowdown in growth was not reflected in the **labour market** in 1998. The second quarter measurement of open unemployment, at the national level, yielded a rate similar to that a year earlier, together with a slight fall in the real wage.

The damage caused by the El Niño climatic phenomenon and the effects of the Asian crisis had a negative effect on export performance, the first by shrinking supply, the second by lowering prices. On top of the marked deterioration in the international price of copper and other metals, which account for two fifths of Peru's exports, came a drastic decline in the volume of products derived from fishing. As a result, the value of merchandise exports fell by about US$ 1.2 billion, whereas imports were down by US$ 200 million, and the merchandise trade balance thus worsened by nearly US$ 1 billion compared to the previous year. Lower payments for services and factor incomes moderated the increase in the current account deficit, which widened to just over US$ 4.1 billion, equivalent to 6.5% of GDP.

The international financial crisis basically affected portfolio investment and some short-term capital flows. However, flows of medium and long-term financing, both foreign direct investment and commercial bank loans held up well. Nonetheless, moderate recourse to **international reserves** was needed to finance the current account deficit.

The Asian crisis also led to the postponement of some importing investment projects in the mining

sector. These included a request by the Shell-Mobil consortium to defer a decision on carrying out the Camisea gas project, in order to strengthen its profitability and improve bargaining conditions with the Government. In the hope of an upturn in copper prices and the resumption of credit lines, feasibility studies were also postponed on the La Granja and Quellaveco copper projects being promoted by the Cambior and Mantos Blancos companies. For the same reasons, Rio Algom and the Inmet Mining Corporation both put off development of the Antamina copper and zinc deposits.

URUGUAY

The momentum of the Uruguayan economy weakened during the course of 1998. After remaining in the 5% range during the two preceding years, growth picked up to nearly 7% in the first quarter, but later cooled, so that the 1998 growth figure will fail to reach 3%. Against this backdrop, and under a tight fiscal policy, inflation was on the order of 9% for the year, its lowest level in 30 years.

Despite the uncertainty prevailing in international financial markets, deposits in the banking system continued to rise, while the flow of capital from abroad more than covered a widening of the external deficit to the equivalent of 2% of output. The fall in the international oil price brought an improvement in the terms of trade, so that income grew by more than output. By year's end, domestic demand was seen to weaken, unemployment was threatening to breach the 10% level, and a slackening of international trade flows was also in evidence.

Economic policy continued to be focused on bringing about a gradual lowering of inflation, through fiscal policy aimed at balancing public-sector accounts, accompanied by a slowdown in the monthly rate of devaluation. In anticipation of a deterioration in the external scenario, the authorities took further precautionary measures. First they sought to strengthen the banking system and check the

URUGUAY: GROSS DOMESTIC PRODUCT AND INFLATION

(Percentage variation)

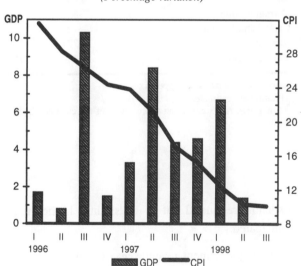

Source: ECLAC, on the basis of official figures.

expansion of credit to the private sector, which had grown rapidly as from 1992. Second, initial steps were taken to set up a US$ 450 million precautionary fund financed by international lending institutions.

Fiscal policy sought to stabilize real expenditure at the previous year's level, in an effort to keep the deficit in 1998 below 1% of output. Fulfilment of this target was satisfactory up to September, although real

URUGUAY: MAIN ECONOMIC INDICATORS

	1996	1997	1998[a]
	Annual rate of variation		
Gross domestic product	5.0	5.1	2.5
Consumer prices	24.3	15.2	9.4
Real wages	0.6	0.2	1.9
Money (M1)	26.4	16.9	24.4
Real effective exchange rate[b]	-0.9	-2.0	-0.6
Terms of trade	-6.1	-1.2	4.9
	Percentages		
Urban unemployment rate	11.9	11.5	10.0
Fiscal balance/GDP	-1.2	-1.3	-1.2
Real deposit rate	3.1	3.9	5.7
Real lending rate	54.0	48.9	47.2
	Millions of dollars		
Exports of goods and services	3 847	4 256	4 310
Imports of goods and services	3 974	4 450	4 590
Current account	-233	-321	-430
Capital and financial account	386	721	580
Overall balance	153	400	150

Source: See the statistical appendix.
[a] Preliminary estimates.
[b] A negative rate signifies an appreciation of the currency in real terms.

expenditure turned out to be slightly higher than anticipated.

Central government revenue was up by 8% in real terms during the first seven months of the year. The expansion of credit facilities bolstered private consumption, especially automobile purchases, and this contributed to increased revenues from value added tax, specific taxes and customs duties. The contribution of public-sector enterprises was also considerable. Meanwhile, expenditure increased less than revenue.

The economic programme called for a drop in the rate of devaluation of the national **currency** to a range of

7%-9% annually. In line with this target, the monthly devaluation rate was cut from 0.8% to 0.6% in April, and at the same time the width of the exchange-rate flotation band was narrowed from 7% to 3%.

Under this exchange rate system, monetary growth depended on the quantity of money demanded by the public, who increased their real balances. In the 12 months ending September, money expanded by 16%, including a real increase of about 6%. There was a larger real increase in local currency deposits (10%), with that of foreign currency deposits (17%) in dollars more vigorous still.

After initial rapid growth, **gross domestic product** lost momentum beginning in the second quarter. Final demand continued to expand actively in the first quarter, in the context of a rise in real family income, an expansion of bank credit and solid demand for non-traditional exports. But later, consumption slowed, discouraged by the rise in interest rates, uncertainty as to the future trend of the economy and the application of Central Bank provisions aimed at strengthening the solvency of the banking system. In this regard, capital and asset requirements were raised and loan oversight requirements were tightened. Exports, already harmed by the downturn in certain international prices, began to feel the effects of lower demand from abroad.

Generally speaking, following a first quarter of active expansion **productive sectors** experienced ups and downs which were felt in nearly all services and in industry, although the performance of the various subsectors differed. Construction grew moderately, boosted by significant public infrastructure investment. In the second half agricultural output managed to recover from the setback suffered as a result of weather problems in the first half of the year; the output of beef cattle increased, as did milk production. Transport and communications, meanwhile, continued to expand.

In early 1998 the **unemployment rate** fell to 10%, a figure one and a half percentage points below its mid-year level in 1997. Recent measurements, however, have detected an upward trend in unemployment with simultaneous rises in activity and employment rates. Real wages posted accumulated growth of about 2% in the first nine months of the year.

Strict compliance with the goals of the financial programme helped to ensure that the main economic policy target was met by bringing **inflation** down to a single-digit annualized rate. As in previous years, consumer prices in private education and health services rose most rapidly, whereas textile and clothing prices fell back, under strong competition from imports. The stability of fuel and lubricant prices helped to keep transport price hikes below average.

The **external deficit** widened slightly, to 2% of GDP. The balance-of-payments current account deficit was slightly larger than anticipated, owing in particular to a decline in revenues from tourism. Despite the international financial turbulence, Uruguay had no problem financing this deficit and continuing to build up its international reserves, for which it had the support of an investment grade rating granted to its

sovereign debt. In a recent US$ 150 million bond issue the risk premium went up slightly to 345 basis points.

Merchandise exports increased by 4.5%. Trends in the different categories varied: while traditional products fell back, sales of non-traditional goods grew strongly. There was a significant increase in gross automobile exports to the region; sales of rice, meat and fish were also substantial, the improvement reflecting chiefly to the rise in their prices. In contrast, the value of exports of wool and textile products and of leather and leather products suffered sharp contractions. The impact of the international crisis on buyer countries affected Uruguayan exports to Asia, which fell back by one third, and those destined for Brazil, which stagnated, while sales to Argentina increased significantly.

Merchandise imports also grew, albeit more slowly. The purchase of consumer and capital goods continued to expand at a rapid pace (10%), while the value of oil and gas imports declined by 40%, owing to the sharp drop in the international price of petroleum.

VENEZUELA

In 1998 the Venezuelan economy suffered the full impact of the drop in the price of oil, the country's main source of income, a trend aggravated by the repercussions of the international financial crisis. As a result, deficits were generated in the fiscal accounts and on the current account equivalent to over 4% and to 1.5% of GDP, respectively, in contrast to the surpluses achieved the previous year. These imbalances created pressure on the bolívar, which the Central Bank of Venezuela successfully countered by using its abundant international reserves and raising domestic interest rates. The higher cost of money, the public spending cuts undertaken to rein back the fiscal deficit, a slackening of exports and the uncertainty aroused by legislative and presidential elections at the end of the year all combined to erode the economic upturn that had begun the previous year and turned it into

VENEZUELA: GROSS DOMESTIC PRODUCT AND INFLATION

(Percentage variation)

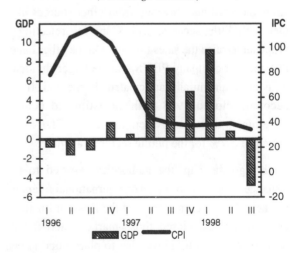

Source: ECLAC, on the basis of official figures.

recession. It is estimated that gross domestic product for the year as a whole will suffer a decline on the order of 1%. Inflation continued to slow, held in check by the recessionary climate and by the scant nominal depreciation of the bolívar, although annualized inflation remained above 30%.

Economic policy was directed towards dealing with the impact of external events by trying to moderate their effects on macroeconomic equilibria. The fight against inflation took priority, at the expense of the economic recovery that had begun the year before. In the sphere of structural reforms, Congress approved the establishment of a macroeconomic stabilization fund to help administer oil earning. On the other hand, the previously announced and important privatization of the aluminium industry had to be postponed.

The **implementation of the budget** was constrained by the sharp contraction in fiscal revenues caused by the collapse in oil prices on the world market. The 1998 budget had been initially estimated on the assumption that the average price of oil exported by Venezuela would be US$ 15.50 per barrel, down from the average of nearly US$ 16.50 obtained in 1997. However, the drop in prices lowered the 1998 average to about US$ 11 per barrel.

Successive downward adjustments to the estimated price were accompanied by drastic budget cuts amounting in all to some US$ 2.3 billion. Attempts to strengthen ordinary revenue from other sources also met with little success, with Congress rejecting a proposal to raise the sales tax rate. On the other hand, the state oil company PDVSA made larger dividend transfers than initially anticipated. In the end, fiscal accounts closed 1998 with an estimated central government deficit equivalent to 4.2% of GDP and a deficit of 5.7% for the public sector as a whole.

To bridge the gap, the authorities resorted to the issuance of debt instruments on international financial markets. However, the onset of the Russian financial crisis in August closed those markets, and it was necessary to wait till November to place bond issues in the German market. In these circumstances, the

VENEZUELA: MAIN ECONOMIC INDICATORS

	1996	1997	1998[a]
	Annual rate of variation		
Gross domestic product	-1.3	5.1	-1.0
Consumer prices	103.2	37.6	31.2
Real wages	-23.3	25.6	...
Money (M1)	88.5	58.4	18.8
Real effective exchange rate[b]	19.2	-22.3	-16.6
Terms of trade	15.6	3.5	-22.8
	Percentages		
Unemployment rate	11.8	11.4	11.2
Fiscal balance/GDP	7.6	2.3	-5.7
Real deposit rate	-34.6	-16.1	8.1
Real lending rate	-26.7	-9.6	19.6
	Millions of dollars		
Exports of goods and services	25 280	25 120	19 225
Imports of goods and services	14 779	18 282	18 570
Current account	8 914	4 684	-1 560
Capital and financial account	-2 230	-1 434	-3 600
Overall balance	6 684	3 250	-5 160

Source: See the statistical appendix.
[a] Preliminary estimates.
[b] A negative rate signifies an appreciation of the currency in real terms.

Government made use of excess funds that had accumulated thanks to the high crude oil prices registered the previous year. PDVSA, in turn, had to cut its budget and issue bonds on world markets.

The Central Bank's **policy of containing inflation** continued to rest on keeping the exchange rate within a band with a central parity devalued as from January at a rate of 1.28% per month, in line with the target set for inflation. This policy was facilitated by the high level of international reserves, particularly when the currency came under speculative attack, especially in May and August. The Central Bank supplemented its intervention in the foreign currency market by placing credit instruments in the money market.

As a result, the exchange rate underwent a nominal devaluation substantially below the inflation rate, which in the end turned out to be higher than anticipated. Another effect of the policy applied by the Central Bank was the gradual raising of interest rates, so that they went up from 15% and 24% on deposits and loans, respectively, at the close of 1997, to as much as 60% and 75% in mid-September, easing down moderately thereafter. This trend finally resulted in positive real rates, after a lengthy period of heavily negative ones.

The use of international reserves, together with lower demand for money, made it possible to contain monetary expansion, which amounted to 12% over the 12 months to the end of November 1998. This partially offset the expansionary effects of the public sector's use of funds accumulated at the Central Bank to make up for the reduction in current revenues. Higher interest rates encouraged placements in savings and time deposits, so that broad money (M2) increased twice as fast as the money supply (M1), but still less than inflation.

Early in the year, the economy kept up the momentum that had enabled it to recover by more than 5% in 1997. In the first quarter of 1998 **gross domestic product** was 9% greater than a year before. In the second quarter, however, growth began to be undermined by cuts in oil exports and public spending following the collapse of oil prices and agreements among producer countries to restrict supply. Private expenditure was also increasingly affected by the downturn, while the real appreciation of the currency and expectations of devaluation diverted a growing fraction of demand toward imports. The result for the year as a whole was that GDP shrank by at least 1%, with similar declines in the oil sector and in the rest of the economy.

Unemployment declined in the first and second quarters, rose again in the third to about 11% and by the end of the year was heading for over 12%. This occurred despite an increase in employment in the informal sector, which in the third quarter accounted for 49% of the actively employed population.

The same factors that adversely affected activity and employment, including the modest nominal depreciation of the currency, helped to moderate **price increases.** This made it possible to end the year with an accumulated annual rate on the order of 31% –still high, but nearly seven points lower than the 1997 figure.

In the first half of 1998 Venezuelan **exports**, affected by the fall in oil prices and shipments, shed one quarter of their previous year's value, and this deterioration persisted during the second half. **Imports**, on the other hand, were up by 10%, driven by the dynamism of the economy at the beginning of the year and by the real appreciation of the currency. The latter factor, reinforced by expectations of devaluation, continued to influence foreign purchases during the second semester and made it possible to smooth out the adverse effect of the economic recession.

These developments eroded Venezuela's typically surplus merchandise trade balance, which shrank to a third, falling below US$ 4 billion. The balance-of-payments current account moved into deficit by nearly US$ 1.5 billion, equivalent to 1.5% of GDP.

In addition to the decline in current earnings there were episodes of capital flight due to lack of confidence in the value of the currency and difficulties in obtaining financing on international capital markets. However, foreign direct investment continued to arrive, totalling about US$ 3.3 billion, thanks to the opening up of the oil industry and the previous year's sale of the State-owned iron and steel company. In the end, the financial account was in deficit by US$ 3.6 billion, and the balance of payments closed with a deficit of over US$ 5 billion. The consequent loss of reserves was staunched by the addition of collateral freed up by the previous year's Brady Bond swap operation. At the beginning of December, reserves amounted to over US$ 14.5 billion, enough to cover more than one year's goods imports.

CENTRAL AMERICA AND MEXICO

COSTA RICA

GDP increased by 5.5%, which was slightly higher than the target figure. The successful performance of the economy was due to a relatively flexible monetary and fiscal policy that sought to stimulate economic activity. The central government's deficit, at 2.9%, was smaller than the previous year's (3.9%), while the external sector's deficit remained almost unchanged (3.6% of GDP). Starting at the end of the third quarter, monetary policy was made more restrictive in order to avert an excessive expansion that might unleash an inflationary process and lead to greater external imbalance.

The Asian financial crisis did not lead to serious problems, thanks to the small size of Costa Rica's capital market and the fact that a large proportion of its exports go to markets that have not yet been affected by the crisis. Nevertheless, the country did not escape the effects of widening interest rate spreads and did experience some capital flight. It benefited, however, from substantial foreign investment and from the export activity of the facilities recently set up in the country by Intel, the microchip manufacturer. The net effect of these factors was a loss of US$ 80 million in international reserves.

Increased economic activity translated into a 23.6% rise in central government revenues in nominal terms. Tariffs were a particularly important contributing factor because of the increase in imports, but higher revenues from income and excise taxes also played a role.

COSTA RICA: MAIN ECONOMIC INDICATORS

	1996	1997	1998[a]
Annual rate of variation			
Gross domestic product	-0.5	3.7	5.5
Consumer prices	13.9	11.2	12.9
Real wages	-2.1	0.8	...
Money (M1)	17.5	43.2	11.8
Real effective exchange rate[b]	-1.0	2.2	0.7
Terms of trade	-5.1	6.0	3.9
Percentages			
Urban unemployment rate	6.6	5.9	5.4
Fiscal balance/GDP	-5.2	-4.0	-2.9
Real deposit rate	3.1	1.6	-0.6
Real lending rate	11.0	10.2	8.0
Millions of dollars			
Exports of goods and services	4 861	5 472	6 600
Imports of goods and services	5 036	5 723	6 765
Current account	-109	-329	-375
Capital and financial account	54	545	295
Overall balance	-55	216	-80

Source: See the statistical appendix.
[a] Preliminary estimates.
[b] A negative rate signifies an appreciation of the currency in real terms.

The central government's expenditures rose more slowly than revenues, and the deficit (3.9% of GDP in 1997) consequently fell to 2.9% in 1998. The consolidated public sector's deficit was 3.1% of GDP. This was due to the fact that the central bank's losses were not totally offset by the customary surplus posted by public enterprises and decentralized institutions, which narrowed this year owing to higher expenditures for investment.

Nonetheless, the improvement seen in public accounts is primarily attributable to the upturn in economic activity rather than to the solution of problems of a more structural nature, such as the inflexibility of expenditure entailed by the public sector's commitments in relation to the service on the domestic debt, pension payments and the required outlays for tax credit certificates.

During the first eight months of the year, monetary aggregates expanded more than planned (total liquidity increased 13.3% between January and September), and this, along with low interest rates, provided a strong stimulus for economic activity. The combined effect of these low rates and the reductions made in reserve requirements –until they settled at 15% in March 1998– was to generate an abundant supply of credit in the economy, particularly for the private sector, where the rise for the year was over 30%. Credit for the public sector, on the other hand, followed a much more moderate trend, growing by 4.4%.

Meanwhile, the lag in interest rates was also reflected in a stronger preference on the part of the general public for dollar-denominated deposits.

The exchange rate was devalued 12% during the year, i.e., around a point and a half below inflation, under a crawling peg regime.

With regard to the level of economic activity, the 16.3% boom in investment in real terms was the greatest force driving the economy, while exports of goods and services also showed much more strength than in previous years, rising 13% at constant prices. These two variables were strongly influenced by investment and by the start-up of Intel's foreign sales. Gross fixed investment not only increased in the

private sector, but also rose in the public sector, where it had been subject to heavy restrictions prior to 1997.

The manufacturing sector grew at a real rate of 7.4%, exceeded only by construction and some services, such as electricity and water, transport, storage and communications. In manufacturing as well as construction, the greater availability of domestic credit at lower interest rates had a positive effect, as did the influx of foreign investment into the country's export processing zones (EPZs).

The agricultural sector, on the other hand, though it performed better than in 1997, recorded real growth considerably below the GDP rate of 3.2% due to extremely adverse weather conditions that affected the harvests of several important crops. During the first six months of the year the effects of El Niño hurt basic grain crops and the livestock industry, but traditional agricultural exports actually benefited. On the other hand, in October traditional crops (coffee in particular) were seriously damaged by Hurricane Mitch.

The consumer price index (CPI) increased at a pace slightly above the previous year's (12.9% as opposed to 10.7% as of October when measured year-on-year). This can be attributed to some degree of demand pressure, given the quickening pace of economic activity and the economy's abundant liquidity. The CPI would have risen more had it not been for the downturn in fuel prices.

The two increases in minimum wages made during the year amounted to a rise of 14% in this indicator in nominal terms, which translated into a slight wage increase in real terms.

Unemployment fell as the economy expanded. A significant portion of new job creation was probably due to the strength of the labour-intensive construction sector, which saw a rapid expansion.

Exports increased by 23.9%, while imports, though very strong owing to the expansion of the economy, rose less steeply (19.3%), and the country therefore had a more favourable merchandise trade balance than the year before.

The export activity of Intel was what contributed the most to the upturn in exports (as well as imports). Exports from the EPZs (including Intel's external sales) rose 80% between January and September in comparison with the previous year.

The services trade balance showed an improvement over the previous year thanks to the performance of the tourism industry, which expanded by 15%. The current account balance was very similar to the previous year's, although it did take a slight turn for the worse, chiefly as a result of the level of interest payments and other external expenditures by the private sector.

Reserves fell 25% between December 1997 and the end of September 1998 (from US$ 1.141 billion to US$ 910 million), but then recovered most of the ground they had lost. This was due primarily to the outflow of private capital, since the level of capital inflows, particularly in the form of foreign direct investment, was even higher than in 1997. The outflow of capital was attributable to a preference on the part of the private sector for dollar deposits outside the country, since for the greater part of the year, domestic interest rates were lower than those available abroad.

EL SALVADOR

GDP expanded by 3.5% in 1998, which was very close to the 1997 rate. Its growth was driven principally by non-traditional exports, a sustained increase in remittances from family members residing abroad and maquila operations, even though coffee exports fell sharply (31%) owing to a decline in international prices. Although the strong increase in imports was reflected in a large deficit on the current account, reserves rose considerably, and it is estimated that the fiscal deficit will amount to 1.6% of GDP.

Inflation stayed at very low levels during almost the entire year. Nevertheless, the sharp increase in prices in November (2.2%) contributed to a 4.3% rate for the period November 1997-November 1998.

Inflows of foreign capital increased substantially, and the resulting high level of liquidity facilitated the growth of the credit supply, a reduction in interest rates and the continuing stability of the exchange rate. Gross fixed investment increased at a faster pace than the year before, especially in the public sector.

El Salvador, like Guatemala, Honduras and Nicaragua, was hit hard by Hurricane Mitch, which damaged both export crops and the livestock industry.

It is expected that the hurricane's greatest impact on economic activity will be felt in 1999.

In 1998, the basic objectives of **economic policy** remained the same as before: to maintain price and exchange-rate stability and to bolster the stability of the financial system. Under a policy aimed at maintaining a **fiscal balance**, the deficit rose slightly to 1.6% of GDP. The current revenues of the non-financial public sector through September 1998 were up by 11.5% over the same period for the previous year as the result of a 7.2% increase in revenue from income and value added taxes and a 33.1% increase in non-tax revenues. Current expenditures of the non-financial public sector rose 12.2%, driven in large part by increases in consumption and gross investment. Current savings rose by 140.2 million colones, thanks to which there was an overall surplus (including grants and donations) of almost 500 million colones. Capital expenditures rose 6.8% as the result of an increase in gross investment.

Monetary policy was, as before, geared to regulating liquidity and reducing gluts in order to maintain stability and ward off inflationary pressures. Up through the third quarter, inflows of foreign capital generated an upswing of 12.1% in liquidity (as

EL SALVADOR: MAIN ECONOMIC INDICATORS

	1996	1997	1998[a]
	Annual rate of variation		
Gross domestic product	2.0	4.0	3.5
Consumer prices	7.4	1.9	4.3
Money (M1)	17.5	-1.9	7.7
Real effective exchange rate[b]	-7.8	-0.3	-1.0
Terms of trade	-14.4	15.5	2.5
	Percentages		
Urban unemployment rate	7.5	7.5	7.2
Fiscal balance/GDP	-2.0	-1.1	-1.6
Real deposit rate	6.2	9.7	7.7
Real lending rate	10.6	13.9	12.4
	Millions of dollars		
Exports of goods and services	2 203	2 706	2 740
Imports of goods and services	3 466	3 885	4 340
Current account	-99	97	-235
Capital and financial account	264	267	635
Overall balance	165	364	400

Source: See the statistical appendix.
[a] Preliminary estimates.
[b] A negative rate signfies an appreciation of the currency in real terms.

measured by M3) over the same period in 1997, with a more pronounced rise being observed in foreign-currency and time deposits. Nominal deposit and lending rates for both domestic and foreign currency fell throughout the year. The economy's high liquidity led to an expansion of credit, especially for construction and housing (23%), services (25%) and the agricultural sector (10%). In 1998, as in the previous two years, the exchange rate held steady thanks to intervention by the Central Reserve Bank and the sterilization of excess inflows of dollars through open market operations.

The aim of the **tariff reduction programme** was to reach a floor rate of 5% and a ceiling of 10% for intermediate goods and of 15% for final products. (Tariffs on raw materials and capital goods had already been lowered to zero as of December 1996.) Accordingly, in July 1998 the rate for intermediate goods subject to a 10% tariff was lowered to 7%; the rate for intermediate goods subject to a 15% tariff was reduced to 12%; and the rate for final products subject to 20% tariff rates was set at 17%. In addition, a free trade treaty with the Dominican Republic was approved which is to enter into effect in January 1999.

An important step forward in the area of **structural reform** was the start-up of the country's five new pension fund management boards (AFPs), whose operations are based entirely on domestic capital. Another highly significant event was the amendment of the law under which the Fund for the Economic and Social Development of Municipalities (the FODES Act) had been created, which, starting this year, calls for an annual allocation from the central government of 6% of the national budget's gross current revenues. The Free Zone and Marketing Act was also modified in an effort to protect sensitive sectors of the national economy, particularly agriculture.

Economic activity was buttressed by the buoyancy of the external sector (including the *maquila* industry), rising FDI (especially in connection with the purchase of State-owned enterprises), the growth in credit for the various sectors of the economy and a decline in interest rates.

All sectors of the economy turned in positive performances. The sectors showing the strongest growth included construction (3.7%), mining (5.5%), and manufacturing (7%). Agriculture remained the slowest-growing sector (0.2%). Salient features in the construction sector were the development of public infrastructure, with a focus on health, education, marketing and urban roadways. In the private sector, housing, hotels and agricultural projects were the most active areas. Outstanding performances in the manufacturing sector were posted for sugar (9.5%), clothing (7.2%), metal products (7.2%) and non-metallic minerals (7%).

The **employment** situation improved in 1998. The number of workers registered with the Salvadoran Institute of Social Security was up by 7.3% in July 1998 as compared with July 1997. According to multi-purpose household surveys, the urban unemployment rate averaged 7.2% from May to October, compared with 7.5% during that period in 1997.

The National Minimum Wage Council ordered a 9% nominal increase in the minimum **wage** starting in May. This was the first increase since July 1995.

The **current account deficit** for the year is estimated at close to US$ 240 million. Nevertheless, thanks to the country's abundant inflows of hard currency in the form of foreign investments and loans, the overall balance showed a surplus of US$ 400 million.

In the first nine months of the year, a **trade deficit** of US$ 1,044,500,000 was recorded, which was 11.8% above the figure for the corresponding period of the preceding year. On the one hand, exports rose by only 2.2% —as opposed to the 35% increase registered the previous year— due to the decline in coffee sales (-30%). Nevertheless, *maquila* exports continued to post high rates of growth (17.7%), as did sales of non-traditional products to markets outside of Central America (24.9%). On the other hand, imports expanded 18%, an increase over the 16% figure registered in 1997.

Trade with the rest of Central America slowed. Exports grew 7.2%, whereas the previous year's figure was 25%, while imports rose only 4.8%, versus the previous year's 14%.

As of September, copious inflows of foreign exchange had boosted net international reserves to close to US$ 1.8 billion, or 41% above the 1997 level.

Foreign direct investment has been one of the key factors in the economy. As of October it had reached US$ 867.7 billion thanks to investments by recently privatized energy-distribution companies and telecommunications firms.

GUATEMALA

GDP grew 4.5% in 1998, a figure slightly above the previous year's rate (4.1%). The adoption of more expansionary monetary and fiscal policies and the continuing strong performance of the export sector were influential factors in this regard. The relative stability of the nominal exchange rate and favourable trends in import prices, particularly for oil, resulted in an annual inflation rate that was within the range anticipated by the authorities.

One of the main factors influencing Guatemalan society in 1998 was the need to move forward with the implementation of the peace accord. On the other hand, the adverse effects that Hurricane Mitch and El Niño had on the country during the year were compounded by the international climate of uncertainty engendered by the crisis in financial markets. In addition, the local financial system was shaken by a liquidity crisis in the second half of the year.

Progress was made during the year in implementing the agreements contained in the peace accord. The major portion of a planned divestiture of assets was accomplished with the completion of the process involved in privatizing the State's electricity and telecommunications companies.

Gross capital formation increased slightly faster than the year before (16.4% versus 15.2%), in part thanks to new investment projects in both the public and private sectors.

For the third year in a row, economic policy was not supervised by the International Monetary Fund, since the failure to arrive at an agreement on tax issues prevented the conclusion of a stand-by arrangement.

GUATEMALA: MAIN ECONOMIC INDICATORS

	1996	1997	1998[a]
	Annual rate of variation		
Gross domestic product	3.0	4.1	4.5
Consumer prices	10.9	7.1	7.4
Money (M1)	12.8	31.3	18.1
Real effective exchange rate[b]	-4.8	-5.0	-0.1
Terms of trade	-30.3	26.4	5.3
	Percentages		
Unemployment rate	3.7	5.0	5.9
Fiscal balance/GDP	-0.1	-1.1	-1.6
Real deposit rate	-2.9	-1.5	-0.3
Real lending rate	10.7	10.9	10.1
	Millions of dollars		
Exports of goods and services	2 767	3 175	3 685
Imports of goods and services	3 534	4 187	4 980
Current account	-391	-547	-700
Capital and financial account	567	834	900
Overall balance	176	287	200

Source: See the statistical appendix.

[a] Preliminary estimates.

[b] A negative rate signifies an appreciation of the currency in real terms.

Monetary policy was generally expansionary. The timetable for lowering the reserve requirement which had been approved in late 1997 was put into operation, and the 24.6% requirement in effect in December 1997 had thus been reduced to 19.6% by June. In addition, the authorities continued with their policy of refraining from engaging in open market operations, and net placements of financial instruments used for purposes of monetary regulation were actually negative. On the other hand, the amount of credit extended by the Banco de Guatemala to the Government was slightly lower in net terms. Liquidity in the banking system consequently rose rapidly,

expanding at an annualized growth rate of more than 24%.

By the fourth quarter of the year, however, a lack of liquidity in the banking system had become evident. This may have been due to excessive haste on the part of financial institutions in placing the fresh resources that had become available, which in turn may have led to a deterioration in the quality of their portfolios. To forestall any major problems, the authorities decided to inject additional liquidity into the system, and by early December the liquidity squeeze appeared to be under control.

All the main sectors of activity benefited from the availability of additional credit. Commerce, consumption, and other areas received 54% of the new funds, while industry and agriculture, taken together, received 23%.

Quasi-money deposits were down, and a tendency to substitute dollar deposits for local-currency deposits was in evidence. The average deposit and lending rates remained at much the same levels as those seen at the end of 1997, and spreads stayed in the neighborhood of 10 points.

Fiscal policy also showed signs of an expansionary stance, with the central government's deficit increasing from 1.1% of GDP in 1997 to 1.6% to 1998. On the other hand, owing to the authorities' decision to cease open market operations, quasi-fiscal losses fell from 0.5% to 0.2% of GDP. Government expenditure again rose sharply (27%), in part because of the need to fulfil commitments made in connection with the peace accord.

Public finances exhibited their customary vulnerability in the area of tax revenues. The peace accord called for a tax take of 10% in 1998, but the level actually reached was barely 9.1%. Consequently, a decision was made to modify the timetable for the achievement of fiscal targets. A more balanced approach to the use of direct and indirect taxes was also adopted as a means of correcting the Government's tendency towards an over-reliance on indirect taxes. Nonetheless, preliminary data for 1998 point to an increase in the level of indirect taxes.

The country's new Tax Administration Superintendency (SAT) became operational in 1998.

The nominal **exchange rate** registered a moderate devaluation (4.6%). In order to ward off greater pressures on the currency, the authorities decided to draw upon the country's international reserves. As a result, the Banco de Guatemala's net sales of dollars for the year amounted to US$ 408 million.

Guatemala's electricity company (EEGSA) and telecommunications firm (GUATEL) –the country's two largest State-owned enterprises– were **privatized**. The new postal system also began operation under private management. In addition, progress was made in drawing up the necessary plans for the privatization of the country's main airports and ports. Plans for rehabilitating the railroad lines for which concessions had been awarded in 1997 were delayed, however.

The **economy** grew 4.7% in 1998, a higher rate than in the preceding year (4.1%). Both the agricultural sector and manufacturing expanded at a rate of 3%. The mining sector maintained its elevated growth rate, thanks to the results for oil production and exploration, while the construction sector grew 9.5%. With respect to total supply and demand, the substantial increase in the pace of gross capital formation and the favourable trends observed in public and private consumption account for the sectoral patterns that materialized.

The relative stability of the exchange rate allowed the country to post a November-to-November **inflation** rate of 7.4% despite the steep rise in prices registered in November (2.65%) as a consequence of Hurricane Mitch.

The **employment** situation showed some improvement over the course of the year. Nevertheless, the impacts caused by Hurricane Mitch when it hit Guatemala in November 1998 included massive unemployment in some parts of the country. The **wages** of public-sector employees rose 10%, and a 12% increase in the minimum wage for industrial and farming activities was put into effect.

The deficit on the balance-of-payments **current account** was US$ 700 million, a significantly higher figure than the previous year's US$ 547 million. The result posted on the current account was largely attributable to a marked increase (of more than 50%) in the merchandise trade deficit (US$ 1.423 billion), although this situation was eased somewhat by incoming transfers (US$ 733 million).

The value of exports climbed at a slower rate (8.9%) than in 1997 (16%). Imports, however, increased significantly (20%) for the second year in a row (22% in 1997) in response to rising liquidity, the growth of the economy and the relative stability of the exchange rate.

The public external debt rose from US$ 2.135 billion in 1997 to US$ 2.248 billion in 1998. The service on the external debt amounted to US$ 214 million.

Net international reserves trended downward in the course of the year, although they were boosted by the receipt of US$ 512 million in revenues from the privatization of EEGSA in September.

HONDURAS

Economic growth in 1998 amounted to 2.8%, which was below both the figure for 1997 and the 5.6% rate that had been projected by the authorities at the start of the year. During the first 10 months, the economy was spurred by the steps taken to cut taxes and stimulate competitiveness and productivity, which *fuelled private domestic investment and consumption demand. Meanwhile, a prudent management of monetary policy held inflation to moderate levels until October (14.5%), although it then rose considerably in the last two months of the year.*

HONDURAS: MAIN ECONOMIC INDICATORS

	1996	1997	1998[a]
	Annual rate of variation		
Gross domestic product	3.3	4.3	3.0
Consumer prices	25.3	12.7	15.1
Money (M1)	27.3	33.6	17.7
Real effective exchange rate[b]	1.6	-5.3	-7.9
Terms of trade	-12.9	29.2	7.6
	Percentages		
Urban unemployment rate	6.5	6.4	5.8
Fiscal balance/GDP	-3.8	-2.8	-3.5
Real deposit rate	-7.0	8.1	1.2
Real lending rate	3.5	17.7	11.6
	Millions of dollars		
Exports of goods and services	1 911	2 187	2 385
Imports of goods and services	2 118	2 472	2 880
Current account	-188	-191	-295
Capital and financial account	294	404	230
Overall balance	106	213	-65

Source: See the statistical appendix.

[a] Preliminary estimates.

[b] A negative rate signifies an appreciation of the currency in real terms.

Exchange-rate policy provided for the continued use of a crawling peg, and the existing policies for the liberalization of trade and promotion of foreign investment were maintained.

Late in October, in what proved to be the worst catastrophe in its entire history, Honduras was devastated by Hurricane Mitch. Preliminary estimates put the figures at 5,600 people dead, 8,000 people missing and approximately two million people injured or otherwise affected. A vast number of homes were ruined, nearly a third of the road network was damaged and a large number of bridges were destroyed. Extensive areas of farmland were damaged as well. As a result, the growth of the economy and exports slumped. Small businesses and microenterprises also sustained damage to inventories and facilities.

Estimates for the last two months of 1998 and at least part of 1999 indicate that both output and per capita income will drop, open unemployment will rise and productivity will decline. In addition, the external imbalance is expected to worsen due to a decline in exports and an increase in imports of food and building materials, among other things.

The fiscal deficit swelled to 3.5% of GDP in spite of the fact that, during the first 10 months of the year, the policies in effect had brought about such a notable improvement in public finances that fiscal accounts were showing a surplus as late as the end of the second quarter.

The new Administration approved the Production, Competitiveness and Human Development Promotion Act as a means of encouraging foreign and domestic investment and spurring job creation. Income tax cuts that lowered the rate from 42% to 25%, a reduction in export taxes and a gradual decrease in the wealth tax were approved. Customs duties on imports of raw materials and capital goods were also reduced. To offset the effect of these measures on tax revenues, the value added tax (VAT) was raised from 7% to 12%. The slackening of economic activity during the last two months of the year brought about a slight decline in tax revenues as a percentage of GDP. The deficit was financed chiefly with foreign funds.

Spending policy had two objectives: to curb the growth of expenditure while at the same time increasing the proportion of social spending (particularly on education and nutrition); and to promote agricultural activity, especially export crops. Government spending rose 18%, but real investment in social programmes was lower than in 1997.

The authorities' flexible exchange-rate policy tended to overvalue the lempira slightly but did not significantly affect the country's competitiveness. Up to October, the lempira had depreciated 3.4%. In March the central bank widened the exchange-rate band around the reference rate used for dollar auctions to 7%.

Implementation of the tariff rollback programme continued, and the tax benefits offered in Honduras' free zones were extended to the entire country. The Government signed a free trade agreement with the Dominican Republic and is in the midst of negotiating another such agreement with Mexico.

The main objective of monetary policy was to reduce inflation by attaining greater control over monetary aggregates –and, hence, liquidity– through the use of open market operations. The legal reserve requirement was reduced by two points in April. Credit to the central government continued to drop sharply, but lending to the private sector rose (51%) beyond the high levels of 1997. Lending rates tended to decline, but even so stood at an average of 30% as of September. When the events of November overtook the financial system, it was in the process of toughening up the capital adequacy requirements applying to the nation's banks and portfolios. The general public showed confidence in the system, deposits were maintained and the exchange rate fluctuated only during the first days after the hurricane.

During 1998 the external debt balance rose 2.5% to US$ 4.146 billion. Arrears in servicing the debt amount to 2%. The Government is scheduled to enter into debt-reduction negotiations with the Paris Club with a view to the possibility of obtaining an adjustment in payments or an actual decrease in the balance of its multilateral debt as an essential step towards rebuilding the country.

In April 1998 a regulatory agency was formed to oversee the electricity sector and a bill was submitted to Congress to authorize the partial sale of Hondutel, the State-owned telecommunications company. The Government also plans to license private operators to take over responsibility for service infrastructure at the airports of Tegucigalpa, San Pedro Sula, Roatán and La Ceiba. In addition, the recently formed National Banking Commission stepped up its regulatory and oversight activities. The Secretariat of Tourism was also formed and a new law on police and internal security was enacted.

Spurred by increases in private investment and exports (nearly 4%), the economy performed so well during the first 10 months of the year that, as of September, an annual growth rate of 5.1% was expected.

The destruction caused by the hurricane drove down agricultural production (-1.5%), brought the expansion of government services to a standstill and, generally speaking, curbed the pace of nearly all production activities. GDP growth slowed to 2.8%.

The growth rate for exports of goods and services slumped, as the banana harvests of the last two months of the year were totally lost, as were portions of the shrimp and coffee harvests. Public investment declined due to the downturn of the last two months.

In contrast, construction, which had been displaying tremendous vitality after years of recession, was buoyed further (17%) by the rehabilitation and emergency work required late in the year.

Fiscal and monetary policies contributed to a slower rise in prices in the second half of the year, and the year-on-year rate of inflation as of November was therefore 15%. However, despite the Government's establishment of price controls, it is estimated that the year-end rate will be in excess of 16% due to supply problems.

The nominal minimum wage was raised by 17% at the start of the year. Open urban unemployment declined, falling to 5.8% by March. The *maquila* sector created 9,000 jobs, but in November a short-run decrease in employment amounting to approximately 23,000 jobs was registered.

As of October, the current account deficit was estimated at approximately 2% of GDP. The progress made in this connection was stymied by a drop in exports late in the year due to flood damage, however, and as a result the deficit climbed to the equivalent of 5% of GDP.

Imports were up by 18%, with especially strong increases being seen in imports of machinery, transport equipment and food, although the bill for petroleum products declined. The increase in the external deficit was partially offset by a higher level of incoming private transfers and by inflows of private and banking capital. Even so, the overall balance showed a deficit of US$ 65 million, rather than the increase in reserves that had been expected prior to Hurricane Mitch.

MEXICO

The Mexican economy performed well in 1998, with GDP expanding by more than 4.5%. Nonetheless, this was lower than the rate that had been projected at the start of the year (5.2%); the shortfall was attributable to the fairly unfavourable international economic climate, which was marked by plummeting oil prices and the volatility of short-term foreign capital flows. However, the domestic market remained on its strong growth path, thanks primarily to private consumption and investment. Exports rose, but their growth rate continued to slip, and higher imports resulted in an external deficit of 3.6% of GDP. Until the start of the third quarter, there were no reports of any fundamental changes in Mexico's financial markets, but in late August and early September pressure on the exchange rate began to build; in large part this was due to the deepening international crisis, which was reflected in larger outflows of financial capital and greater constraints on access to foreign funding. As the year drew on, government spending was adjusted downward and monetary policy became more restrictive. The exchange rate underwent a steep depreciation and inflation climbed, overshooting its target rate by six points.

The chief aims of **economic policy** were to promote economic growth and employment –within the limits set by the severe constraints affecting the economy– and to reduce inflation through support for sound public finances and a flexible monetary policy capable of coping within the present adverse international economic environment.

The **public-sector deficit** rose to 1.4% of GDP (0.4% in 1997) as budgetary revenues fell by 9% in real terms owing to the sharp downturn in oil revenues. The 36% drop in the price of crude oil exports on the

MEXICO: GROSS DOMESTIC PRODUCT AND INFLATION
(Percentage variation)

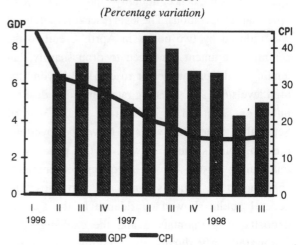

Source: ECLAC, on the basis of official figures.

international market drove down public-sector income by more than 1% of GDP. Tax revenues showed a real increase of 8.6% thanks to the higher level of economic activity and the adoption of various measures for improving tax collection. In the third quarter, income tax receipts rose 8.7%, revenues from the VAT climbed 10.3% and revenues from the special taxes levied on production and consumption jumped 51.2%. On the other hand, non-tax revenues (–28.9%) reflected the drop in oil prices. As a result, government spending was adjusted on three different occasions during the year to offset this decrease in revenues. The 3.1% decrease in funded discretionary expenditures in real terms was a reflection of cutbacks in capital expenditure, whose impact could be seen in the level of investment in the communications, transport and energy sectors, although current spending rose. In spite of these adjustments, social spending accounted for a larger proportion of total expenditure than before,

MEXICO: MAIN ECONOMIC INDICATORS

	1996	1997	1998[a]
	Annual rate of variation		
Gross domestic product	5.5	7.0	4.5
Consumer prices	27.7	15.7	17.4
Real wages	-11.1	-0.6	1.6
Money (M1)	39.6	29.4	15.0
Real effective exchange rate[b]	-11.0	-13.3	-1.5
Terms of trade	2.76	0.0	-2.6
	Percentages		
Urban unemployment rate	5.5	3.7	3.3
Fiscal balance/GDP	-0.1	-0.4	-1.4
Real deposit rate	-2.0	-0.8	-2.5
Real lending rate	...	...	...
	Millions of dollars		
Exports of goods and services	106 901	121 701	129 200
Imports of goods and services	100 060	122 109	137 400
Current account	-2 330	-7 449	-15 500
Capital and financial account	4 104	17 959	16 500
Overall balance	1 774	10 510	1 000

Source: See the statistical appendix.
[a] Preliminary estimates.
[b] A negative rate signifies an appreciation of the currency in real terms.

and this increase was particularly marked in the case of programmes designed to reduce extreme poverty. Non-discretionary expenditure declined 10% in real terms thanks to the fact that interest payments, commissions and other expenses related to the public-sector debt fell 15.2%.

The external **public debt** reached US$ 92 billion, 4.2% more than the balance as of December 1997. In the first half of the year, the public and private sectors underwrote more than US$ 5 billion on international markets on relatively favourable terms, thus counteracting the contraction of capital flows to equity and money markets. Issues then declined in the third quarter as conditions in international markets

deteriorated. However, towards the end of the year the Government carried out more than US$ 6 billion in financial operations, with half of these transactions taking the form of Pemex credits and debt issues and the other half being loans to the federal government.

In a departure from the course taken in 1997 and from what had originally been planned for 1998, **monetary policy** was tightened in response to the volatility displayed by financial markets. The use of a floating exchange rate and adjustments in interest rates were the main methods used to contend with the instability of international financial markets. Faced with the departure of capital from the country and a steeper depreciation of the peso, the monetary authorities also began to create a liquidity squeeze in order to oblige financial institutions to maintain a short daily position with the central bank. This mechanism was brought into use in March, with the central bank leaving the money market short 20 million pesos per day, but by December the figure had been raised to 130 million pesos per day. All of this exerted upward pressure on interest rates. In addition, the Banco de México decided to ask commercial banks for a deposit of 1.25 billion pesos per business day until reaching an accumulated amount of 25 billion pesos. This helped to drive up the interbank interest rate, which reached approximately 40% by September (about 20% in real terms).

The exchange-rate regime based on the **flotation of the currency** coped fairly well with the volatility of the international financial market and, as a result, the peso depreciated sharply, with an especially steep downturn being observed for a short time in late August. Consequently, the nominal appreciation of the dollar during the first 11 months of the year amounted to 25% (8% in real terms). This financial volatility had no major impact on the net international assets of the Banco de México, which totalled US$ 21.7 million as of the end of November, or 9% more than at the end of 1997.

The financial indicators of the **banking system** showed that it had high, although declining, delinquency rates. For the first time since 1995, credit showed signs of a rebound in real terms. The upward trend in non-performing loans had also come to an end, and loan-loss provision and capitalization indices were recovering. The rise in interest rates in August again had an impact in terms of the constraints on bank financing and put pressure on loan portfolios by increasing the risk that debtors might stop repaying their loans, which would result in another upswing in delinquency rates. This situation created uncertainty as to what sort of methods would have to be used to come up with a lasting solution to the problems of the country's savings deposit insurance fund (Fondo Bancario de Protección al Ahorro, also known as Fobaproa). The bill that the executive branch sent to Congress in March to authorize the conversion of these liabilities into public debt was not approved until 13 December and was heavily amended. The debt assumed by the public sector totalled 610 billion pesos (US$ 60 billion).

The index of prices and quotations on the Mexican stock exchange trended downward, with a particularly marked slump beginning in the third quarter; the cumulative decrease for the first 11 months of the year amounted to 30% (36% in real terms and 44% in dollars). The steep slide in quotations was one of the reasons for the sharp reduction in the level of Mexican securities held by foreign institutional investors.

The executive branch sent various bills to Congress designed to carry forward the **reform of the financial system**. These bills would: (i) put the Banco de México in charge of exchange-rate policy; (ii) give autonomy to the National Banking and Securities Commission and strengthen its regulatory and oversight functions within the financial system; (iii) eliminate restrictions on foreign investment in the financial system; and (iv) consolidate Fobaproa's debt with the public debt of the federal government. Following a round of international bidding, the Government awarded US$ 116 million worth of operating concessions for a number of airports as part of its **privatization** programme. Bids were also received for the Morelos petrochemical complex, and

it is expected that the successful bid will be announced in early 1999.

The main stimuli for growth came from domestic demand, which rose steadily; particularly strong upswings were seen in private consumption (7%) and investment (15%). On the other hand, the agricultural sector's GDP declined 1.6% in the first nine months of 1998 due to the effects of the droughts affecting the country during the first half of the year, which were followed by heavy rains in important farming areas; as a result, it was necessary to resort to an unusually high volume of basic grain imports (corn, beans, sorghum and wheat). The other sectors of activity in the economy expanded. Industrial production rose 7.1% in the first nine months of the year, with the manufacturing sector turning in the most dynamic performance thanks to the growth of the *maquila* industry. The automotive industry increased its output by 7% in the first 10 months of the year; this was chiefly attributable to the expansion of the domestic market (40%) since exports dropped 3%. The construction industry grew 5%, which was half as much as in 1997. The services sector also experienced widespread increases in activity. In particular, commercial establishments' retail sales rose 10% in the first 10 months of 1998.

Inflation continued to decline until mid-year, but the devaluation of the peso caused it to overshoot the official target of 12%; the overall figure for 1998 is estimated at 18%. Real wages made significant gains, the first since 1994. In addition, a 14% increase in the minimum wage took effect in December.

The open **unemployment** rate was 3.1% in October, which was virtually the same as the figure for October 1997 (3.2%). In the first 10 months, the number of workers registered with the Mexican Social Security Institute increased by 860,000 to 13.6 million. In the *maquila* sector, employment climbed by 10% in the first nine months of the year, bringing the total number of persons employed in that sector to over 1 million in September.

The **current account** of the balance of payments showed a deficit of US$ 15.5 billion (3.6% of GDP), which was twice as much as in 1997. Transactions on the merchandise account slowed, but the trade deficit increased considerably, reaching US$ 7.4 billion. Exports of goods rose 6%; non-oil exports were up 11% but oil exports plunged 35% due to plummeting prices, and the terms of trade therefore took a turn for the worse. With a growth rate of 13.5%, imports also lost some of the momentum they had displayed in 1997. The capital and financial account yielded a surplus of US$ 16.5 billion (8% less than in 1997). On the one hand, total foreign investment amounted to US$ 8.5 billion, or 50% less than in 1997. Portfolio investment slid from US$ 5.037 billion to US$ -800 million, while direct investment was US$ 9.3 billion, or US$ 3 billion less than the year before. On the other hand, public and private liabilities and other short-term capital movements amounted to US$ 7.7 billion, and international reserves were US$ 1 billion higher than they had been in December 1997.

NICARAGUA

The robust recovery the Nicaraguan economy had been experiencing slackened in 1998 as gross domestic product grew by 3.6%, a lower rate than the authorities had anticipated at the start of the year (6%). The performance of the economy was undermined by Hurricane Mitch, considered the worst natural disaster in the country's recent history, which took a high toll in human lives, property losses and damage to the environment. The preliminary estimate of property damage is US$ 900 million; of that figure, 94% represents damage to capital assets and 6% direct production losses.

In this situation, inflation more than doubled (18%). In the fiscal sphere, major progress was made in putting public finances on a sound footing. Foreign investment continued to flow into the country, supporting the process of remonetization and expanding the monetary aggregates, especially deposits in foreign currency. The exchange rate held to the announced rate of crawl, so that the córdoba depreciated in real terms in the face of higher inflation.

The natural disaster badly affected the export sector. However, with international grants and inflows of private funds from abroad, it was possible to finance a consistently high current account deficit.

Since 1997 **economic policy** has been oriented primarily toward narrowing a large external gap, and

NICARAGUA: MAIN ECONOMIC INDICATORS

	1996	1997	1998[a]
	Annual rate of variation		
Gross domestic product	4.8	5.0	3.5
Consumer prices	12.1	7.3	17.9
Real wages	-2.1	-0.2	7.7
Money (M1)	25.9	30.7	18.4
Real effective exchange rate[b]	2.2	4.7	2.0
Terms of trade	-8.09	-5.9	6.3
	Percentages		
Unemployment rate	16.0	14.3	12.2
Fiscal balance/GDP	-1.5	-1.5	-0.1
Real deposit rate	-1.2	1.7	0.3
Real lending rate	6.1	13.1	10.0
	Millions of dollars		
Exports of goods and services	807	867	800
Imports of goods and services	1 300	1 608	1 645
Current account	-698	-813	-805
Capital and financial account	215	820	640
Overall balance	-483	7	-165

Source: See the statistical appendix.

[a] Preliminary estimates.

[b] A negative rate signifies an appreciation of the currency in real terms.

to reforming and modernizing the State. In March 1998 the Government of Nicaragua signed an agreement with the International Monetary Fund for a new Enhanced Structural Adjustment Facility for the period 1998-2000 to achieve sustainability in its public finances and external sector and continue with structural reform.

In April the Consulting Group for Nicaragua announced the commitment of donor countries to provide financial assistance of US$ 1.8 million during the period 1998-2000, earmarked for a programme to accelerate growth and reduce poverty.

Combatting poverty was recognized as crucial for maintaining political and social stability and was made a key part of the Government's strategy, which placed high priority on modernizing the rural sector, planning investments in rural infrastructure, creating loan funds for small farmers and expanding and improving social services.

The Government's **fiscal programme** sought to increase public saving significantly and make the public sector more efficient by modernizing State institutions and expediting the privatization of public utilities such as electricity and telecommunications. Thanks to the implementation of tax reform in 1997 and greater efficiency in the government Administration, it is estimated that the central government deficit will decrease from 1.5% to 0.1% of GDP.

Monetary policy was restrictive in order to neutralize the increase in bank liquidity caused by inflows of foreign capital. Although the increase was less than that posted the year before, the liquidity of the economy expanded in all respects, especially due to the increase in deposits in foreign currency.

With the change adopted in 1997 in the way in which negotiable investment certificates (CENIS) were issued, in 1998 it was possible to control the amounts issued and reduce the discount rate; the latter action brought about a slight drop in deposit and lending rates.

The **foreign exchange policy** remained unchanged, with daily crawl of the parity with respect to the dollar, resulting in a 12% devaluation in nominal terms.

Under current conditions, the Government of Nicaragua is committed to preserving a sound **economic policy**, in other words, to maintaining the country's financial stability and making progress in structural reforms, with only a few minor adjustments. However, it hopes to reduce its external debt and obtain new financing.

In 1998, according to preliminary official data, GDP increased only 3.6%, owing to the destructive effects of Hurricane Mitch, compared with the 6% that had been expected at the start of the year.

The **agricultural sector** grew by 3.4%, compared to 8.9% the previous year, in large part owing to the agricultural losses incurred during the last three months. It is estimated that the losses in the harvest of annual crops (bananas, sesame, soybeans, peanuts and tobacco) represented 43% of total agricultural losses, coffee and sugar cane 13% and other agricultural products (fruits and vegetables) 14.4%.

Growth in production of farmed shrimp slowed from its rate of 11% in 1997 to 1.5%, because of major damage to the industry's stock of capital assets.

It is estimated that **industrial activity** increased only 1.8%, rather than the 2.8% anticipated, owing to problems in supplying agricultural and fishing inputs for the food processing industries.

Tertiary activities expanded by 3.3%, less than the expected rate of 4.1% because of the destruction of the country's infrastructure.

It is estimated that **construction** grew by 6.6%, in part because of the momentum it exhibited until September and in part because of the initial work of reconstruction begun in the last two months of the year.

The year-on-year **inflation** rate (November-November) rose nearly 18%, disappointing expectations throughout most of the year that the rate would be around 10%. The shortage of agricultural products caused by the El Niño weather phenomenon and subsequently by Hurricane Mitch explains the rise in prices.

As an annual average, open **unemployment** declined owing to the growth of employment, especially in primary and secondary activities. However, a major increase in unemployment is anticipated by the end of the year, although it could be partially offset by the start of reconstruction activities. During the first eight months, the average real wage in the formal sector rose considerably, in large part reflecting pay increases for central government employees, while wages in the private sector grew moderately.

It is estimated that the large **current account** deficit declined from US$ 814 million to US$ 805 million, chiefly owing to lower interest payments and increased family transfers from abroad. Although grants from abroad and foreign investment continued to increase, the current account deficit was financed largely with international reserves.

The trade deficit in goods f.o.b. widened by US$ 110 million (16.5% more than the figure for 1997) as a result of a decrease in exports (13%) and a slight increase in imports (1.4%).

Merchandise exports declined because of the major reduction in non-traditional exports, in spite of growth in exports of traditional items, chiefly coffee, shrimp, lobsters and molasses.

On the other hand, there was an increase in imports of consumer goods, especially durables, and of capital goods. In contrast, imports of intermediate goods declined, owing to the lower cost of oil, despite increases in purchases of raw materials for manufacturing and construction.

In 1998, most of the existing external debt was duly serviced. At the end of September 1998, Nicaragua's external debt totalled US$ 6.28 billion.

PANAMA

In 1998 gross domestic product grew by 3.5%, compared to 4.7% in 1997. This change reflected a fall in agricultural output and a decline in activity in the Colón Free Zone owing to lower demand from its usual Latin American customers; growth in other economic activities was satisfactory. Investment remained highly dynamic, as in 1997, partly owing to increased public spending, while expanded credit helped to sustain consumption growth.

The central government fiscal deficit increased, although the financial imbalance for the public sector as a whole was small. The September-to-September inflation rate was 0.8%; the unemployment figure remained at 13.4%; and real wages increased in a number of sectors.

The main **economic policy** objectives of previous years remained unchanged in 1998: modernization

and reform of the State through privatization, external debt reform and trade liberalization.

The goal of **fiscal policy** was to maintain financial balance in the public sector. Central government revenue grew by 5%, but expenditure increased even more, producing a deficit of 4% of GDP. However, thanks to the profits of State-owned enterprises and entities, the overall deficit was only 0.7% of GDP.

Receipts from indirect taxation were up by 15% as of October, while those from direct taxes fell by 5.5%, partly because taxation on income within the Colón Free Zone was eliminated. Overall central government spending expanded by 26.5% in the first half of the year, with an exceptionally large increase in capital expenditure (119%) due to infrastructure investment (highway construction and repair and urban road works).

PANAMA: MAIN ECONOMIC INDICATORS

	1996	1997	1998[a]
	Annual rate of variation		
Gross domestic product	2.7	4.4	3.5
Consumer prices	2.3	-0.5	1.5
Terms of trade	0.10	10.5	-1.8
	Percentages		
Urban unemployment rate	16.7	15.4	15.6
Fiscal balance/GDP	-1.7	-0.6	-4.0
	Millions of dollars		
Exports of goods and services	7 510	8 440	8 540
Imports of goods and services	7 501	8 605	8 965
Current account	-159	-309	-595
Capital and financial account	442	786	1 195
Overall balance	283	477	600

Source: See the statistical appendix.
[a] Preliminary estimates.

The government external debt rose to US$ 5.35 billion, 6% more than in 1997, and the cost of debt servicing was reduced to US$ 460 million, half as much as the previous year, as a result of major debt repayments. In April, the Government placed a US$ 300 million bond issue on international markets (maturity of 10 years at a rate of 8.875%). The proceeds were used to redeem Brady bonds with a face value of US$ 71 million and to help finance the public budget.

The **trade liberalization policy** begun in mid-1997 was strengthened in January 1998. Tariffs were cut to a maximum of 15% and a minimum of zero, apart from special rates for motor vehicles (15%-20%), rice (49%) and milk (50%). In addition, 50% of the shares in electric power generation and distribution companies were sold off, for a total of US$ 603 million.

Deposits attracted by the international banking centre in the first nine months of the year were up 6.4% compared with the same period in 1997. These additional resources made possible a considerable increase (18.1%) in domestic credit, especially for commerce (22%), personal consumption (25.8%), finance and insurance (62%) and mortgages (10%). The foreign loan portfolio grew by 3.1%, with particularly large increases in credit to North America (41%) and Central America (19%), whereas there was a reduction in lending to South America (4.6%).

Operations in the Colón Free Zone slowed, with a 2.7% decline in re-exports and an increase of only 1.4% in imports, owing to reduced demand from Colombia, Ecuador and Venezuela.

During the 1997-1998 fiscal year the number of transits through the Panama Canal fell by 1%, but the average size of the ships increased, as did the volume of cargo transported. Income was up (11%) owing to a new increase in rates and charging for deck cargo. Container cargo handling in the Balboa and Cristóbal ports also increased substantially, and the numbers of tourists and their average spending in the country rose.

Agricultural production suffered a setback for the second consecutive year (1%). There was a substantial drop in banana production owing to the effects of a prolonged strike and the lower quota imposed by the European Union. Adverse weather conditions also led to reduced output of fruit and vegetables and basic grains. On the other hand, livestock production improved, particularly pigs and poultry, as did catches of shrimp and fish.

The **manufacturing sector** grew by 5% while adapting to trade liberalization. Production increased in the categories of foods and beverages, rubber footwear, publishing, and glass and glassware; there was also increased output of cement (24% to September) and metal products. The petroleum refinery resumed operations, and output in the first half of the year rose by 34.2%. There were setbacks in other areas, however, including tobacco, paper products, leather footwear and wearing apparel.

Over the first 10 months of 1998 **consumer prices** in Panama City rose by only 1.5%. This modest increase reflected falling prices in transport and communications and furniture and household furnishings and fittings, but there were significant price increases in medical and health care and in recreation, education and cultural services. Wholesale prices also fell by 4.4% in the first nine months, owing to lower prices for imports (6.5%) and industrial products (3.5%).

Employment rose by 3.2% between August 1997 and August 1998, but the open unemployment rate stayed at the same level, owing to an increase in the economically active population, as reflected in household surveys. There were considerable improvements in nominal wages in the first half of the year: 3.6% in manufacturing, 3.2% in hotels and restaurants, and 2% in other services.

The country's **foreign trade** slowed considerably in 1998. Combined export and import flows were barely 1% higher, compared to 14% in 1998; this was mainly due to reduced merchandise demand from Latin America. In terms of financial flows, considerable foreign direct investment continued, attracted by the privatization of electric power companies.

Re-exports from the Colón Free Zone totalled US$ 4.36 billion during the period from January to September, 2.4% less than in the same period in 1997. Imports, on the other hand, totalled US$ 4.07 billion for those nine months, an increase of 1.4%. Merchandise volumes were 3.4% and 4.3% higher, respectively.

A 6.5% increase in domestically-produced exports is expected for the year as a whole (US$ 702 million). Banana sales were down 28%, but this was made up for by increased exports of refrigerated fish and shrimp, coffee, clothing and petroleum products.

Imports for the domestic marke rose by 7% (US$ 3.203 billion); there were increased purchases of foodstuffs, various intermediate goods and, above all, capital goods. The value of petroleum purchases was 30% lower than in the first nine months of 1997.

THE CARIBBEAN

BARBADOS

The Barbados economy continued to perform well in 1998, experiencing economic growth for the fifth consecutive year. Overall growth in the economy is expected to be on the order of 2%, with inflation of approximately 0.2%. For the calendar year, the fiscal deficit is projected to be US$ 57.4 million, some 2.5% of gross domestic product The balance-of-payments current account is expected to produce a reduced surplus of some US$ 5.5 million, as domestic exports have declined, reflecting a contraction in sugar earnings.

Growth in tourism is expected to be around 6% by the end of 1998, although the decline in performance observed in the third quarter is expected to continue into the fourth quarter of the year. Manufacturing should show a slight improvement over the previous year despite mixed fortunes in 1998. According to projections, real growth in non-tradables will be sustained by strong activity in the private sector, especially in construction.

Government policy in 1998 was characterized by increased emphasis on social services, a comprehensive poverty eradication programme, direct support for businesses in non-traditional sectors and the creation of financial schemes to assist the working poor. The value-added tax system (VAT), which provided for zero rating on a number of basic commodities, established a direct correlation between the incidence of the tax and expenditure on consumption, thereby reducing reliance on the system of direct income taxation. VAT opened a window of

BARBADOS: MAIN ECONOMIC INDICATORS

	1996	1997	1998[a]
	Annual rate of variation		
Gross domestic product	5:1	3.0	2.0
Consumer prices	1.8	3.6	0.2
Real effective exchange rate[b]	-0.6	-5.8	1.7
	Percentages		
Urban unemployment rate	16.4	14.5	12.1

Source: See the statistical appendix.
[a] Preliminary estimates.
[b] A negative rate signifies an appreciation of the currency in real terms.

opportunity for service activities that could be undertaken by small and medium-sized enterprises that did not qualify to pay VAT.

The upward trend in investment in 1997 continued into 1998, strengthening the country's capacity to generate foreign exchange and sustainable employment over the medium and long term. Careful management of the substantial economic gains registered in the first three quarters of 1998 continued to assist in the financing of the Government's parallel initiatives to underwrite social progress. The pace of foreign exchange reserve accumulation moderated somewhat, and the fiscal deficit widened as a result of Government's commitment to its social policy.

In the first nine months of the year, the **economy** continued to register strong growth with low inflation and a further reduction in unemployment. Real GDP rose by an estimated 4%, significantly faster than the average growth rate of 2.9% for the corresponding period in the previous five years. In order to avoid overheating the economy, the Government announced plans to slow down its capital works programme. Growth continued to be led by the non-tradables sector, with construction providing the impetus and new job opportunities; the private sector's contribution to the industry consisted mainly in residential construction and tourism-related and commercial infrastructure projects. Increased employment in tourism and manufacturing helped to reduce the unemployment rate in 1998.

With respect to **agriculture**, cane fires during the crop season and drought during the planting season in 1997 reduced sugar production by 25.9% in 1998. The drought extended into 1998 and contributed to a fall in production of milk and food crops. Fish catches recovered by 28.3% in 1998, while poultry production increased by 2.8%.

The **construction** sector grew by some 13.2% in the first nine months of 1998 –almost twice the rate for the corresponding period of 1997. Activity in this sector was dominated by public sector works. Quarrying and other construction-related subsectors increased output by 40.1%.

For the second consecutive year, **manufacturing output** increased during the first nine months. Growth was estimated at 5.7%. Food processing output rose by 4.3%, while the production of beverages increased by 10.9%. A contraction of 12.7% in the output of electronic components was recorded, continuing the declining trend which began in 1992 and continued unabated thereafter, except in 1996, when output increased by 6.5%. Declining production was also observed in the chemical (5.5%) and the garment (24%) industries. The oil refinery, which had been refining domestic crude obtained through secondary recovery practices and a large proportion of imported crude, ceased operations in February 1998.

The wholesale sector recorded growth of 6.5% in 1998, as it responded to strong demand for imports and the overall favourable performance of the tourist industry.

Tourism continued to be the fastest-growing earner of foreign exchange and recorded its highest level of growth, estimated at 7%, compared with the first nine months of each year since 1994. In spite of a slowdown in long-stay arrivals during the third quarter, total arrivals between January and August rose by 8.9%. The vulnerability of the sector's international competitive position was highlighted when the inauguration of cheaper flights from the United Kingdom to South-East Asia was reflected in a slight contraction in arrivals from that country, especially in July. The sector also faced increased competition from some Mediterranean routes, resulting in a 2.0% decline in the number of cruise ship passenger arrivals.

At the end of September 1998, the annual rate of **inflation** stood at 0.2%, a significant drop from the 7.2% observed over the corresponding period in 1997. This was due in part to the zero rating of some food items in the implementation of the VAT system. Lower prices were recorded for food items, fuel and electricity, household utilities and supplies, and clothing and footwear, while retail prices increased for all other categories.

In spite of a modest expansion in the labour force, the **unemployment** rate declined to 12.1% at mid-year 1998 as compared with a rate of 14.5% at mid-year 1997.

The **current account** of the balance of payments was in surplus at US$ 41.9 million, the lowest recorded for the nine-month period in the previous six years, when the surpluses averaged US$ 96.5 million. A 50% contraction in export earnings from sugar contributed to the decline in earnings from domestic exports. Retained imports increased by 11.7% with significant increases in outlays on electronic components, construction materials, textiles and machinery. These negative influences on the current account balance were partially offset by earnings from services, which increased by 13.4%, mainly as a result of increased earnings from tourism (12.7%) and from transportation services. Net capital inflows moderated

to US$ 11.4 million from a figure of US$ 14.6 million for the corresponding nine-month period of the previous year.

CUBA

Gross domestic product (GDP) declined for the second consecutive year (1.5%) owing in large part to the fall in sugar production (3.2 million tons). Limited access to capital markets continued to have an adverse effect on the economic situation. The balance-of-payments current account deficit again widened (US$ 300 million) mainly as a result of the worsening imbalance in the trade in goods and services. Current transfers (family remittances and grants) increased, while the amount of factor services remained the same as in the previous fiscal year. The capital account surplus (US$ 290 million) proved insufficient to finance the current account deficit, further eroding the already scant international reserves.

Earnings from international tourism and telecommunications continued to expand, as did family remittances and foreign investments, all of which helped to ease the island's serious foreign exchange shortage. On the other hand, the terms of trade improved significantly.

Drought in the eastern provinces and damage caused by Hurricane George generated extraordinary expenditure of some US$ 630 million, or the equivalent of 2.6% of GDP. In addition, the negative impact of the economic embargo on the Cuban economy over the last 37 years was estimated by government authorities at US$ 60 billion.

Economic policy continued to be geared towards securing the foreign currency required to restore production levels and basic services to the population. At the macroeconomic level, the priority objectives have been to achieve fiscal balance, reduce the accumulated monetary liquidity and curb inflation.

CUBA: MAIN ECONOMIC INDICATORS

	1996	1997	1998[a]
	Annual rate of variation		
Gross domestic product	7.8	2.5	1.5
	Percentages		
Unemployment rate	7.6	6.8	6.5

Source: See the statistical appendix.
[a] Preliminary estimates.

The fiscal deficit widened to 2.5% of GDP, compared with 2% in the previous year, owing to a greater increase in expenditure (2.9%) than in revenue (1.9%). Revenue from the circulation and sales tax improved by 3.6%, but the tax on services declined by 7.5%. Increases were recorded in revenue from taxes on profits (29.4%) and on use of labour (27.2%).

On the expenditure side, current expenditure increased (4.3%), while capital expenditure fell (-4.8%). The Government continued to accord priority to basic services to the population, and hence increased current expenditure on social assistance (32.6%), housing and community services (16.8%), public health (7.1%), social security (5.3%) and education (3.9%). Current expenditure on defense and public order was cut by 1.3%, reflecting the savings and austerity measures imposed by the Government in response to the current economic crisis.

The Central Bank pursued its policy of restricting both local currency credits and use of foreign currency in the public sector. It succeeded in maintaining the monetary base at virtually the same level as in the previous year (equivalent to 39% of GDP).

Rates on local-currency savings deposits remained unchanged, and, after adjustment for inflation, proved negative. On the other hand, attractive yields on foreign-currency savings accounts lured savers, making more funds available for productive purposes. The banking system disbursed over US$ 500 million in short-term loans to be used as working capital for businesses.

An important aspect of structural reform has been the treatment of foreign capital, which continued to flow in 1998, under the new Foreign Investment Act of 1995. By mid-year, 340 joint ventures involving foreign capital had been set up. In the real estate sector, 10 joint ventures had been established with foreign capital for the construction and remodeling of buildings for offices, housing, commercial establishments and related services. The semi-public enterprise, Corporación Financiera Habana, was set up by the Spanish credit institution, Caja Madrid and the Banco Popular de Ahorro de Cuba, to finance business activities. Another semi-public enterprise, Health de Cuba was formed by a British firm, Health, and a Cuban company. In the electricity sector, two joint ventures were set up involving French and Canadian capital to modernize the electricity generating plants and use gas for generation.

In 1998 Cuba became a full member of the Latin American Integration Association (LAIA) and was admitted as an observer to negotiations on the new Lomé Agreement between the African, Caribbean and Pacific (ACP) countries and the European Union.

In terms of output, the best-performing sectors were tourism (20%), mining (7%) and construction (4%). Agricultural output was down (-3%), and growth in manufacturing production slowed (2.5%).

International tourist arrivals increased to 1.4 million persons, representing gross revenue of US$ 1.9 billion. The hotel occupancy rate rose to 60% from 55% in the previous year.

Mining expanded for the fifth consecutive year (7%) as a result of the increase in nickel production (8%). The fall in agricultural output was linked mainly to the further decline in sugar cane cultivation, while cattle farming and non-cane crops showed no clear signs of recovery. The gross fish catch again increased by 14%, under the new management and worker incentive system.

Construction also expanded, buoyed by the development of tourism infrastructure, new housing starts and building repairs. Oil production increased to 1.7 million tons, which facilitated a slight increase in electricity generation.

The consumer price index rose by 5% as a net result of higher prices on the informal market and lower prices for agricultural products and government food services. Controlled market prices were maintained at virtually the same level as in the previous year.

The average nominal wage rose by less than the rate of inflation, but incentives in convertible pesos and foreign currency were extended to 1.4 million workers in high priority activities such as tourism and the energy sector. The rate of unemployment declined from 6.8% in 1997 to 6.5%; it was highest among young women in the eastern provinces.

Stronger growth in imports compared with that of exports caused the trade deficit in goods and services to widen. The higher value of merchandise imports reflected increased volumes purchased, since international prices dropped. Food imports, in particular, increased in volume.

Merchandise exports fell owing to a decline in international prices. Sugar exports were down both in volume and price, while nickel exports expanded in volume but traded at weaker international prices. In contrast, tobacco sales (US$ 300 million) and fishery products expanded substantially.

The value of sales in foreign currency on the formal domestic market went up by 15% (US$ 800 million); Cuban products accounted for a higher percentage in 1998: 44%, as against 41% in the previous year.

The external public debt increased to US$ 10.2 billion, much of that in the form of short-term loans at high interest rates. The Banco Nacional de Cuba

rescheduled its approximately US$ 750 million of commercial debt owed to 28 Japanese firms.

HAITI

In 1998, output grew by close to 3%, marking an improvement over the preceding year, although results sector by sector were very uneven. Progress was made in restoring macroeconomic equilibria: inflation slowed to 8.2%, the fiscal deficit narrowed to 1.2% of gross domestic product, and the rate of exchange stabilized at 16.9 gourdes to the dollar. However, these results, attributable to strict monetary discipline, conceal the difficulties entailed in giving continuity to the structural reforms of the economy –initiated two years ago– and to the pending project of boosting economic recovery after the embargo. Investment expanded by over 7%, mainly as a result of government activity.

With more than five quarters elapsed since the Prime Minister's resignation and with the cutback in external cooperation disbursements due to the failure to pass the State investment budget, the Government had to resort to a provisional arrangement with the International Monetary Fund (IMF) to promote stability and pursue some reforms and projects already underway. This "Shadow Program" for fiscal 1998 was subject to strict monitoring, on a quarterly basis, of its growth, inflation and fiscal expenditure targets, among others.

Fiscal policy was characterized by efforts to put public finances back on a sound footing by increasing tax receipts (12.6%) and curbing expenditure, which increased by only 4.7% compared with the previous year. In this way, the fiscal deficit was brought down, in relative terms, to 1.2% of GDP.

Failure to secure parliamentary approval for the budget and a lack of external financing due to the freeze on a major portion of external cooperation disbursements continued to constrain the

HAITI: MAIN ECONOMIC INDICATORS

	1996	1997	1998[a]
	Annual rate of variation		
Gross domestic product	2.8	1.1	3.0
Consumer prices	14.6	15.6	8.2
Real effective exchange rate[b]	-15.0	-14.1	-7.5
Terms of trade	-6.6	8.3	2.8
	Percentages		
Fiscal balance/GDP	-1.6	-2.0	-1.2
	Millions of dollars		
Exports of goods and services	257	289	300
Imports of goods and services	782	801	720
Current account	-73	-77	-110
Capital and financial account	24	117	105
Overall balance	-49	40	-5

Source: See the statistical appendix.
[a] Preliminary estimates.
[b] A negative rate signifies an appreciation of the currency in real terms.

Government's operations throughout 1998. However, the availability of domestic financing allowed for an increase in capital expenditure greater than in previous years. Fiscal improvement was due in part to containment of the wage bill, thanks to a voluntary retirement programme which 1,555 civil servants opted for.

Monetary policy tended to be restrictive. Although deposits in local currency and in dollars expanded by 11.4% and 20.5%, respectively, monetary authorities were prudent in handling liquidity, again issuing 91-day bonds of the Banque de la République d'Haïti at nominal rates of 27% towards the middle of the fiscal year. Only credit to the Government expanded (by almost 700 million gourdes) on the basis of the agreement in effect since the previous year to combine the current expenditure and investment budgets.

Despite a renewed preference for dollar deposits, strict control of the monetary variables and the increase in interest rates on local-currency deposits shored up the nominal exchange rate, stabilizing it at an average of 16.85 gourdes to the dollar, just 2% above the previous year's rate. This, combined with an inflation rate averaging 12.7%, signified an appreciation of the local currency against the dollar.

Structural reforms had been suspended since the previous year following the Prime Minister's resignation and could not be resumed on account of the continuing political crisis. As a result a number of State enterprises still await modernization through privatization, capitalization or concession, and these happen to be the largest and most important companies in terms of their economic impact: the telephone company, the electricity company, the sea ports and the airport. Reform of fiscal accounts and the design of a regulatory framework for modernizing the State apparatus are some of the first measures that will be needed to revitalize the economy.

With respect to **economic activity**, the agricultural sector performed well (3.8%), since the pattern of rainfall was favourable and Hurricane George occurred in late September after the harvest. Construction (7.5%) was boosted by public works, road-building and irrigation infrastructure in the rural areas and some residential building. A slowdown was noted in the remaining sectors except for the financial sector and the *maquila* industry, which achieved more vibrant growth than in the previous year.

Public works and imports of equipment prompted by the appreciation of the Haitian gourde account for the recovery in gross domestic investment (7.4%) following two years of decline. However, this

dynamism did not extend to domestic industry, which continued to lose momentum.

The easing of exchange-rate pressures contributed to a reduction in **inflation**. The annual average was 12.7%, but towards the end of the fiscal year the slackening in prices was more pronounced, and inflation subsided to 8.2% in relation to September of the previous year. This was partly due to the good harvests of some basic crops and to falling prices for petroleum products.

The **minimum wage** continued to stagnate in nominal terms, while wages paid in agriculture and in the urban informal sector are believed to have been forced down by pressure from the large number of unemployed. Moreover, the unemployment situation deteriorated further.

The **trade deficit** –US$ 265 million as at June 1998– widened further (close to 10%), compared with the previous year. While the value of exports had increased by 55% at the close of the third quarter of the fiscal year, this was not sufficient to offset the sharp increase in imports of foodstuffs, vehicles and various manufactures during the last quarter. The expansion in exports was led by the *maquila* garment industry and traditional products such as coffee, cocoa and sisal, while it is estimated that imports consisted largely of manufactured consumer goods, since purchases of capital equipment increased little.

Service transactions are expected to show a decline due to the continued slump in tourism. In addition, the current account deficit is expected to have widened following the decrease in private remittances from abroad, notwithstanding a slight decline in debt service payments on the external debt.

Prudent fiscal management and the achievement of the targets set under the IMF Shadow Program suggest that foreign currency reserves may have attained US$ 157 million at the end of September.

JAMAICA

Data for the first half of 1998 showed the Jamaican economy turning in a sluggish performance, but for the full year GDP is expected actually to decline (-3.5%). Both monetary and fiscal instruments were used to contain inflation, the latter with mixed results. Excess liquidity was absorbed by Central Bank open market operations, and the declaration of a tax amnesty served as an incentive to pay up outstanding taxes.

Monetary and fiscal policies have remained consistent with the IMF-endorsed programme. In 1998, the Government fulfilled its commitment to keep prices down in order to avoid a repeat of the high rates of inflation witnessed in the earlier part of the decade. Continued containment of the growth in the money supply, a relatively stable exchange rate and low imported inflation were the strategies used to attain that objective. From the fiscal standpoint, the Government was committed to adjusting expenditure growth in line with emerging trends in revenue intake as a means of reducing the deficit. A tax amnesty was instituted to encourage tax defaulters to pay their outstanding debt, and no new taxes were imposed. The plan was to eliminate the deficit by reductions in government expenditure and restraints on public sector wage increases. However, the deficit as a percentage of GDP is projected to be on the order of 9.3% by the end of 1998. This compares with an estimate of 6.8% recorded in 1997.

Generally, **economic activity** was sluggish during the first half, with growth estimated at 0.2%. **Agricultural production** is estimated to have declined by almost 5% in the second quarter of 1998, in contrast to the 13.5% decline recorded in the corresponding quarter of 1997. The traditional export crop production sub-index increased by 8.9%, mainly because of an increase in sugar cane production, which reflected a shift in the crop cycle associated with drought conditions and postponement of the harvest. By mid-1998, there were indications of a decline of 11% in sugar cane milled and 24.9% in sugar

JAMAICA: MAIN ECONOMIC INDICATORS

	1996	1997	1998 [a]
	Annual rate of variation		
Gross domestic product	-0.5	-2.3	-3.5
Consumer prices	15.8	9.2	10.2
Real effective exchange rate [b]	-15.8	-14.1	-6.0

Source: See the statistical appendix.
[a] Preliminary estimates.
[b] A negative rate signifies an appreciation of the currency in real terms.

produced. The outlook for the whole of 1998 is a shortfall of 18% compared with the production levels of the previous (1996/1997) crop and the lowest output in five years.

The **manufacturing sector** recorded some growth in the first half of 1998, especially in the food processing subsector. The petroleum products subsector declined. Mining and quarrying output for the period January-June 1998 showed an improved performance over the corresponding period of the previous year. Total bauxite production increased by 5.2% to reach 6.3 million tons in direct response to improvements in the management structure of the bauxite company. Total bauxite exports amounted to 6.5 million tons –9.6% more than in the corresponding period of 1997. The sector's total net foreign exchange earnings during the period decreased by 10.5% to US$ 153.7 million, reflecting weak world bauxite prices and depressed demand for alumina, especially in the Asian economies which continued to experience economic difficulties. Alumina prices averaged US$ 177.11 per ton in the second quarter of 1998, down from US$ 192.50 in the corresponding period of 1997.

Construction figures for the first half of 1998 show an improvement compared with the first half of 1997. While installation activity declined, construction activity is estimated to have increased. Cement production increased by 0.9%, compared with 1.4% in the corresponding period of 1997, and sales increased by 19.5%. In 1998, 3,072 housing units were completed, compared to 996 units in 1997, arresting the downward trend seen since 1994.

The financial sector, severely affected by a crisis that peaked in 1997, witnessed the collapse of a number of banks.

Tourism was affected by a prolonged decline in cruise ship passenger arrivals, partly as a result of infrastructure works in Montego Bay. Total visitor arrivals for the period January to June 1998 amounted to 985,429, representing a 1.4% decline when compared with the corresponding period in 1997. In contrast, from January to June 1997, total visitor arrivals increased by 5.9%. For the second quarter of 1998, the overall tourism performance was positive, with a higher number of total visitor arrivals and a 9.5% growth in tourist expenditure compared with the corresponding period of 1997.

A 3% rise in **inflation** was observed in the second quarter of 1998. This was almost entirely due to variations in the transportation and miscellaneous expenses sections of the index. Increases in bus and taxi fares had the most significant impact on the consumer. Inflation was moderate in the other sections of the index. The maintenance of price stability was achieved as the Government strove to meet its goals for the second quarter of 1998.

A decrease in the number of **employment** opportunities, especially in the financial sector, was observed over the first six months of 1998. There was a shift of workers from manufacturing to distribution, as displaced workers turned to less productive occupations, such as retail activities.

The balance-of-payments position improved during the period April to May 1998, as indicated by a US$ 1.4 million increase in net international reserves to US$ 597 million. This represented a turnaround from the decline of US$ 87 million recorded for the corresponding period of 1997. The current account deficit narrowed to US$ 9 million from US$ 60 million in April-May 1997. The capital account balance moved from a deficit of US$ 27 million to a surplus of US$ 10 million. This improvement was assisted by a tight monetary policy, which served to moderate consumer demand, lower inflation and stabilize the foreign exchange market. Within the current account, the surplus on the services account increased by US$ 31 million to US$ 109 million in June 1998. The surplus on the transfers account widened by US$ 1.2 million to US$ 101 million. The deficit on the merchandise trade account contracted by US$ 19 million to US$ 218 million. The smaller deficit resulted from a US$ 45 million decline in imports, which compensated for a US$ 25 million decline in exports. Export earnings for the period stood at US$ 248 million –9.2% lower– due to declines in both traditional and non-traditional exports. Earnings from sugar exports are estimated to have declined by 6.3% from the corresponding period of the previous year. A contraction in demand, mainly from the United States of America, accounted for an 11% reduction in export earnings from wearing apparel. A significant percentage of this market erosion was attributable to the increased competitiveness of production facilities located in East Asia.

A resurgence in private capital inflows, which resulted in an improvement in the balance (from -US$ 1.7 million to +US$ 42.9 million), was primarily responsible for the turnaround in the capital account balance by the end of June 1998.

DOMINICAN REPUBLIC

Economic activity expanded by 7%, which was slightly less than anticipated owing to the damage caused by Hurricane Georges. The fiscal account showed a small deficit (-0.6% of GDP) and this, too, was due to the effect of the hurricane on capital and current expenditures, although these higher outlays were partially offset by an increase in the tax take. In addition, year-on-year inflation declined to 5% as compared to 8% in 1997.

The main impetus for growth came from the demand for gross domestic investment (25%) and domestic consumption (19%). The increase in investment originated to a large extent in the construction sector, which, in addition to other stimuli, received a boost from the reconstruction work needed to repair the damage to infrastructure caused by the hurricane. Unrequited current transfers continued to climb and this, in combination with the increase in the government payroll, fuelled consumption. Among the components of external demand, exports of goods and services from the free zones were quite buoyant, but other exports declined slightly.

The **fiscal year** closed with a deficit (0.6% of GDP) due largely to the effects of Hurricane Georges. Total income rose by 9% and tax revenue by 13%, thanks to administrative improvements and the fact that the consolidation of the exchange rates used for the computation of tariffs had the effect of broadening the tax base for this type of levy, thereby increasing the tax take. Total expenditure rose by 8.7% as a result of increases in capital transfers (46%), current transfers (5.9%) and current expenditure on goods and services (4.8%).

The total public-sector debt stood at US$ 3.47 billion, which was US$ 32 million less than the year before, while interest payments were estimated at US$ 166 million.

Growth of the monetary base and of the narrowly-defined money supply (M1) was slower, reflecting a **monetary policy** designed to reduce excess liquidity

DOMINICAN REPUBLIC: MAIN ECONOMIC INDICATORS

	1996	1997	1998[a]
	Annual rate of variation		
Gross domestic product	6.8	8.2	7.0
Consumer prices	4.0	8.4	4.8
Real effective exchange rate[b]	-6.5	2.4	7.3
Terms of trade	-3.9	4.4	0.9
	Percentages		
Unemployment rate	16.5	15.9	14.3
Fiscal balance/GDP	-0.4	0.8	-0.6
	Millions of dollars		
Exports of goods and services	6 287	7 197	7 510
Imports of goods and services	6 611	7 574	8 440
Current account	-240	-225	-505
Capital and financial account	201	458	500
Overall balance	-39	233	-5

Source: See the statistical appendix.
[a] Preliminary estimates.
[b] A negative rate signifies an appreciation of the currency in real terms.

through open-market operations. This pushed interest rates up. Broad money (M3) expanded by much the same rate as in 1997, since higher interest rates encouraged the substitution of longer-term deposits for cash holdings and since dollars tend to be used as a hedge during bouts of currency speculation. In July 1998, the Dominican authorities unified the official and bank exchange rates at 15.33 Dominican pesos to the United States dollar in a move that cost the Government US$ 16 million.

Important developments in the area of **trade policy** included the free trade treaties signed with the Central American countries and the Caribbean Community (CARICOM), which will enter into force in January

1999. With respect to **structural reforms**, the General Telecommunications Act was passed, and the process of privatizing the State electricity company (the Corporación Dominicana de Electricidad, or CDE) has been initiated. Distribution and generating companies were to be auctioned off towards the end of December.

Led by gross domestic investment (25%), which was a function of the availability of financial resources for the private sector, overall demand grew by 22%, thereby boosting the level of economic activity. In the aftermath of Hurricane Georges, construction activity picked up, thus contributing to the growth of gross fixed investment. Consumption (19%) responded to the increase in real wages and family remittances and to the greater availability of personal loans. Exports of goods and services were up by a modest amount over the previous year's level while imports maintained their growth rate (18%), which was buoyed up by the sustained development of the Dominican economy and by the need to satisfy the demand not met by domestic production.

The devastation caused by Hurricane Georges to vast stretches of the country, and especially to banana, rice and sugar cane plantations, limited growth in the agricultural sector to 0.2%. An upturn in the amount of funds being channelled through the commercial banking system, stable raw material supplies and increased imports of capital goods contributed to an 8% expansion of the manufacturing sector. Stronger demand for garments and an increase in investment inflows sustained an 8% expansion in free zone activities as well. The construction sector maintained its growth rate in 1998 as construction, reconstruction and rehabilitation projects continued apace. In the area of services, the tourism sector posted a growth rate of 6% and was already beginning to recover from the damage caused by the hurricane. The communications industry was the most dynamic sector of the economy (20%) even though the country's principal telephone company sustained losses equivalent to 3% of its assets as a consequence of Hurricane Georges. The

electricity and drinking water sector expanded by 10%.

The lower rate of **inflation** (4.8%) is attributable to the tight monetary policy applied during the year, although the hurricane did lead to some reduction in the supply of several products that carry a high weighting in the basket of staple goods.

The rate of **unemployment** stood at 14.3% (1.6 points less than in 1997). Payroll increases were instituted by the central government, decentralized and autonomous government agencies, and municipalities.

The overall **balance of payments** posted a small deficit (-US$ 5 million). This reflects a current account deficit (-US$ 505 million) which the financial account surplus (US$ 500 million) was not sufficient to offset. The **current account deficit** was double the original estimate owing to the impact of Hurricane Georges. Exports of goods and services were lower than had been projected because of the decline in agricultural sales and in earnings from tourism.

Exports from the free zones, which account for 80% of total exports, were up by 3.2%. On the other hand, exports of domestically-produced goods contracted by 4%, mainly because of falling world ferronickel prices and the decrease in raw sugar shipments made necessary by the reduction in the country's preferential quota for exports to the United States market.

Tariff exemptions approved in late 1997 buoyed up purchases of capital goods and raw materials, thereby contributing to an overall 15% increase in imports. Another contributing factor was the urgent need for supplies during the state of emergency and the start-up of reconstruction efforts. Oil imports were down by 1% owing to the decline in oil prices.

The deficit in investment income widened (8%), but net unrequited transfers expanded by 28%, thus increasing the amount they contribute to the country's foreign exchange inflows by a figure estimated at more than US$ 300 million. The **capital and financial**

account registered a surplus of US$ 500 million. Foreign direct investment increased by US$ 90 million

thanks to the reinvestment of earnings in the tourism sector and new investments in telecommunications.

TRINIDAD AND TOBAGO

On the basis of indicators for the first six months, economic growth for Trinidad and Tobago is projected at 5% for 1998. This would make it the country's fifth consecutive year of positive growth, accompanied by steadily decreasing unemployment rates. The June unemployment figure was 14%, the lowest since 1985. The rate of inflation is expected to be on the order of 6% by year end, compared with a rate of 3.5% in 1997. Growth in 1998 has been generated primarily by the non-petroleum sector, but there has been a sharp decline in agriculture. Gross foreign assets amounted to US$ 1.186 billion at the end of the third quarter of 1998. This represents an estimated import cover of 4.7 months compared with 4.0 months at the end of June 1998.

In 1998, increased foreign investment spurred economic growth, while **economic policy** encouraged local investment and entrepreneurship. Continued emphasis was placed on investment in the petroleum and petrochemical sectors as generators of foreign exchange. At the same time, encouragement was given to small and medium-sized enterprises, especially in the non-oil sectors, to develop and become more competitive in order to break the dependence of the economy on the oil sector. For the fifth year in succession, the economy responded with positive growth and increased employment. Some increase in prices has accompanied this growth and will need to be addressed by policy measures to eliminate the inflation element. It was felt that some aspects of the tax regime, especially the value added tax, may have put a brake on investment at the small and micro-enterprise level. The budget presented in late 1998 for the year 1999 seeks to introduce changes in this area.

For the first nine months of 1998, overall real **economic activity** expanded by 3.3% as a result of

TRINIDAD AND TOBAGO: MAIN ECONOMIC INDICATORS

	1996	1997	1998[a]
	Annual rate of variation		
Gross domestic product	4.5	4.0	5.0
Consumer prices	4.3	3.5	6.3
Real effective exchange rate [b]	-1.3	1.0	-4.6
	Percentages		
Unemployment rate	16.3	17.2	13.4

Source: See the statistical appendix.
[a] Preliminary estimates.
[b] A negative rate signifies an appreciation of the currency in real terms.

improvements in both the petroleum (3.1%) and the non-petroleum (3.3%) sectors. Agriculture and livestock-raising were the exceptions. Activity declined in the third quarter by 0.5% compared with increases of 2.6% and 0.4%, respectively, in the first and second quarters of the year, largely because of a decline in output in the non-petroleum sectors.

In the third quarter of 1998, real value added in **agriculture and livestock-raising** was buoyed by seasonal improvements in the domestic agriculture subsector, which more than offset the declines in sugar and export agriculture; however, for the first nine months of the year, overall real economic activity declined by 17.7% as a result of bad weather conditions and operational problems at the sugar refinery.

While **oil production and exploration** indicators continued to display divergent trends, several positive events during the third quarter, including the discovery of additional hydrocarbon resources, point toward a brighter short-term future for the sector. The completion and commissioning of a refinery upgrade project increased the catalytic cracking capacity of the refinery to 160,000 barrels per day, up from 90,000 barrels per day. For the third quarter, however, refinery throughput averaged 139,100 barrels per day, marginally lower than the previous quarter, and 86% of rated capacity. Exports of crude oil and mineral fuels declined by US$ 2.7 million to a figure of US$ 39.8 million. since international crude oil prices averaged US$ 14.65 per barrel during the second quarter of 1998, down from US$ 15.81 in the previous quarter. Fertilizer production continued to exhibit robust growth in the third quarter of 1998 as a new plant commenced production. By the end of the third quarter, output was 21.4% higher than in the corresponding period of 1997. This expansion in capacity occurred at a time when world prices for fertilizer were declining. Whereas methanol production increased by 31.2% by the end of the third quarter of 1998, world prices fell and exports as well as local sales also fell slightly when compared with the previous quarter.

Manufacturing output continued to decline in the second quarter of 1998, when the index of domestic production dropped by 2.3% compared with a decline of 1.4% in the first quarter. During the entire first semester, output increased by 4.2% compared with 7.6% in the corresponding period in 1997. In particular, declines in food processing, assembly and related products were noted. In the third quarter, however, real output in manufacturing grew by 1.5%. In the **services sector**, increased activity in government and other services contrasted with declines in finance, insurance and real estate (-3.8%); distribution (-14.4%); and transport, storage and communications (-1.1%). These changes contributed to a third quarter decline of 0.5% compared with the second quarter level of output in the non-petroleum sectors.

The **retail price** index rose by 2.4% in the third quarter of 1998, compared with increases of 0.8% and 2.0%, respectively, in the first and second quarters. Higher prices for food, housing, recreation and education accounted for the increase. The annualized rate of inflation to September was 7.1%. Wholesale prices remained stable.

Stronger demand for **labour** by the end of the second quarter brought unemployment down to 13.4%. Year on year, the labour market reflected an improvement: the number of persons with jobs increased by 3.6%. The construction and transport and communications sectors accounted for the major gains in employment, while services and agriculture shed jobs.

For the first half of 1998 the country recorded a **balance-of-payments** deficit of US$ 1.6 million compared with a surplus of US$ 182 million in the corresponding period of 1997. At mid-year 1998, the current account deficit stood at US$ 271 million –a clear deterioration from the figure of US$ 24 million a year earlier. Contributing to this deterioration was a fall-off in net earnings on the merchandise and non-factor services accounts, as the increase in imports in the second quarter outstripped the increase in exports. The current account deficit was not fully financed by inflows of capital, necessitating a drawdown of official reserves. Net capital and financial movements (excluding reserves) resulted in a surplus of US$ 186 million during the second quarter of 1998, following a surplus of US$ 83 million in the previous quarter. The situation was better during the third quarter, when gross foreign assets amounted to US$ 1.186 billion, or US$ 22 million more than at the end of the previous quarter. This figure represents an estimated import cover of 4.7 months as compared with 4 months at the end of June 1998.

STATISTISCAL APPENDIX

Table A-1

LATIN AMERICA AND THE CARIBBEAN: TOTAL GROSS DOMESTIC PRODUCT

(Percentages based on values at 1995 prices)

	Annual growth rates								Average annual rate	
	1991	1992	1993	1994	1995	1996	1997	1998 [a]	1981-1990 [b]	1991-1998
Latin America and the Caribbean [c]	**3.8**	**3.2**	**3.9**	**5.8**	**1.0**	**3.6**	**5.2**	**2.3**	**1.0**	**3.5**
Subtotal (19 countries) [c]	**3.8**	**3.2**	**3.9**	**5.8**	**0.9**	**3.6**	**5.2**	**2.3**	**1.0**	**3.6**
Argentina	10.0	8.9	5.8	8.3	-3.1	4.4	8.4	4.0	-0.7	5.8
Bolivia	5.4	1.7	4.2	4.8	4.7	4.4	4.2	4.5	0.2	4.2
Brazil	1.0	-0.3	4.5	6.2	4.2	2.9	3.0	0.5	1.3	2.7
Chile	7.5	11.6	7.0	5.4	9.9	7.0	7.1	4.0	3.0	7.4
Colombia	1.6	3.9	4.5	6.3	5.4	2.1	3.0	2.0	3.7	3.6
Costa Rica	2.2	7.1	5.8	4.3	2.2	-0.5	3.7	5.5	2.2	3.8
Cuba [d]	-10.9	-11.2	-14.7	0.6	2.4	7.8	2.5	1.5	3.7	-3.1
Ecuador	5.0	3.0	2.2	4.4	3.0	2.3	3.3	1.0	1.7	3.0
El Salvador	2.8	7.3	6.4	6.0	6.2	2.0	4.0	3.5	-0.4	4.7
Guatemala	3.7	4.9	4.0	4.1	5.0	3.0	4.1	4.5	0.9	4.2
Haiti	0.1	-13.8	-2.2	-8.3	5.0	2.8	1.1	3.0	-0.5	-1.7
Honduras	1.8	6.3	7.2	-2.6	5.1	3.3	4.3	3.0	2.4	3.4
Mexico	4.2	3.7	1.7	4.6	-6.2	5.5	7.0	4.5	1.8	3.1
Nicaragua	-0.3	0.8	-0.4	4.0	4.5	4.8	5.0	3.5	-1.5	2.7
Panama	9.0	8.2	5.3	3.1	1.9	2.7	4.4	3.5	1.4	4.7
Paraguay	2.5	1.7	4.0	3.0	4.5	1.1	2.6	0.0	3.0	2.4
Peru	3.2	0.2	5.7	14.7	10.0	2.3	7.4	1.0	-1.2	4.8
Dominican Republic	0.8	6.4	2.0	4.3	4.5	6.8	8.2	7.0	2.4	5.0
Uruguay	2.9	7.4	3.1	5.5	-2.0	5.0	5.1	2.5	0.0	3.7
Venezuela	9.4	6.4	-0.2	-3.0	3.1	-1.3	5.1	-1.0	-0.7	2.2
Subtotal Caribbean [e]	**1.7**	**1.2**	**0.7**	**3.2**	**2.8**	**3.0**	**2.0**	**1.2**	**0.1**	**1.6**
Antigua and Barbuda	4.1	1.0	3.5	4.8	-4.3	5.4	4.6	...	6.1	2.7 [f]
Barbados	-3.5	-5.4	1.0	3.6	2.5	5.1	3.0	2.0	1.1	1.0
Belize	3.2	8.9	4.0	1.6	3.5	3.5	4.4	...	4.5	4.1 [f]
Dominica	2.6	3.0	2.2	2.1	2.3	3.7	2.4	...	4.4	2.6 [f]
Grenada	3.7	1.0	-1.1	3.4	3.0	3.1	4.7	...	4.9	2.5 [f]
Guyana	10.2	11.2	3.1	17.7	2.4	9.2	6.1	...	-2.9	8.5 [f]
Jamaica	0.3	2.5	1.8	1.9	1.7	-0.5	-2.3	-3.5	2.2	0.2
Saint Kitts and Nevis	3.4	3.6	6.7	3.3	3.1	5.6	...	...	5.8	4.3 [g]
Saint Vincent and the Grenadines	0.1	8.9	-0.3	-3.3	8.3	1.0	2.6	...	6.5	2.4 [f]
Saint Lucia	-2.1	7.4	0.4	1.9	4.1	0.8	0.9	...	6.8	1.9 [f]
Suriname	3.5	4.0	-2.2	-7.0	5.0	3.0	5.0	...	0.5	1.5 [f]
Trinidad and Tobago	3.5	-1.1	-1.2	4.2	4.1	4.5	4.0	5.0	-2.6	2.8

Source: ECLAC, on the basis of official figures converted into dollars at constant 1995 prices.
Note: Totals and subtotals do not include those countries for which no information is given.
[a] Preliminary estimates.
[b] Calculated on the basis of figures at constant 1990 prices.
[c] Does not include Cuba.
[d] Calculated on the basis of constant prices in the local currency.
[e] Based on figures at factor cost.
[f] Refers to 1991-1997.
[g] Refers to 1991-1996.

Table A-2

LATIN AMERICA AND THE CARIBBEAN: PER CAPITA GROSS DOMESTIC PRODUCT

(Percentages based on values at 1995 prices)

	Annual growth rates								Average annual rate	
	1991	1992	1993	1994	1995	1996	1997	1998 [a]	1981-1990 [b]	1991-1998
Latin America and the Caribbean [c]	**1.9**	**1.4**	**2.1**	**4.0**	**-1.6**	**1.9**	**3.5**	**0.7**	**-1.0**	**1.7**
Subtotal (19 countries) [c]	**1.9**	**1.4**	**2.1**	**4.0**	**-1.6**	**1.9**	**3.5**	**0.7**	**-1.0**	**1.7**
Argentina	8.5	7.5	4.4	6.9	-4.4	3.0	7.0	2.8	-2.1	4.4
Bolivia	2.9	-0.8	1.7	2.2	2.2	2.0	1.8	2.1	-1.9	1.8
Brazil	-0.6	-1.8	3.0	4.8	2.5	1.4	1.6	-0.8	-0.7	1.2
Chile	5.7	9.7	5.2	3.7	8.3	5.5	5.6	2.4	1.3	5.7
Colombia	-0.3	1.9	2.5	4.3	-3.8	0.1	1.1	-0.1	1.6	0.7
Costa Rica	-0.4	4.4	3.3	1.9	-3.7	-3.2	1.1	2.9	-0.6	0.7
Cuba [d]	-11.6	-11.8	-15.2	0.0	1.8	7.3	2.0	1.1	2.8	-3.6
Ecuador	2.7	0.7	-0.1	2.1	0.8	0.2	1.2	-1.0	-0.9	0.8
El Salvador	0.6	4.8	3.8	3.4	3.6	-0.1	1.9	1.4	-1.4	2.4
Guatemala	1.1	2.2	1.3	1.4	2.2	0.3	1.4	2.0	-1.6	1.5
Haiti	-1.9	-15.6	-4.2	-10.1	-3.1	0.9	-0.8	1.0	-2.4	-4.4
Honduras	-1.2	3.2	4.1	-5.4	2.1	0.4	1.4	0.0	-0.8	0.5
Mexico	2.2	1.8	-0.1	2.8	-7.8	3.7	5.2	2.9	-0.3	1.3
Nicaragua	-3.0	-2.1	-3.3	1.0	-5.4	1.9	2.1	0.8	-3.9	-1.0
Panama	6.9	6.2	3.4	1.3	0.1	0.9	2.7	1.8	-0.7	2.9
Paraguay	-0.4	-1.1	1.3	0.4	1.7	-1.6	-0.1	-2.7	0.0	-0.3
Peru	1.3	-1.6	3.9	12.7	8.1	0.5	5.5	-0.8	-3.3	3.6
Dominican Republic	-1.2	4.3	0.0	2.4	2.7	4.9	6.4	5.3	0.2	3.1
Uruguay	2.3	6.7	2.5	4.9	-3.5	4.3	4.4	1.8	-0.6	2.9
Venezuela	6.8	3.9	-2.4	-5.1	0.9	-3.4	2.9	-3.0	-3.2	0.0
Subtotal Caribbean [e]	**0.8**	**0.3**	**-0.2**	**2.3**	**1.9**	**2.0**	**0.4**	**0.4**	**-0.9**	**0.7**
Antigua and Barbuda	3.5	0.4	2.9	4.1	-4.8	5.4	3.0	...	5.6	2.0 [f]
Barbados	-3.8	-5.8	0.7	3.2	2.5	4.7	3.0	1.6	0.7	0.7
Belize	0.6	6.1	1.4	-1.0	1.8	0.7	2.1	...	1.9	1.7 [f]
Dominica	2.6	3.0	2.2	2.1	2.3	3.7	2.4	...	4.8	2.6 [f]
Grenada	3.5	0.8	-1.3	3.2	2.8	2.7	4.3	...	4.7	2.3 [f]
Guyana	9.4	10.2	2.1	16.6	1.8	8.2	5.0	...	-3.4	7.5 [f]
Jamaica	-0.4	1.8	1.1	1.2	0.1	-1.4	-3.2	-4.4	1.1	-0.7
Saint Kitts and Nevis	3.9	4.1	7.3	3.8	3.6	5.6	...	...	7.0	4.7 [g]
Saint Vincent and the Grenadines	-0.8	7.9	-1.2	-4.1	7.3	0.1	1.7	...	5.5	1.5 [f]
Saint Lucia	-3.4	6.0	-0.9	0.6	2.7	-0.5	-0.5	...	5.3	0.5 [f]
Suriname	2.4	2.8	-3.3	-8.0	2.9	1.8	3.8	...	-0.7	0.3 [f]
Trinidad and Tobago	2.3	-2.2	-2.3	3.0	4.5	3.7	3.1	4.2	-3.9	2.0

Source: ECLAC, on the basis of official figures converted into dollars at constant 1995 prices.
Note: Totals and subtotals do not include those countries for which no information is given.
[a] Preliminary estimates.
[b] Calculated on the basis of figures at constant 1995 prices.
[c] Does not include Cuba.
[d] Calculated on the basis of constant prices in the local currency.
[e] Based on figures at factor cost.
[f] Refers to 1991-1997.
[g] Refers to 1991-1996.

Table A-3

LATIN AMERICA AND THE CARIBBEAN: CONSUMER PRICE INDICES

(December-December variations)

	1991	1992	1993	1994	1995	1996	1997	1998[a]
Latin America and the Caribbean	**199.6**	**417.2**	**882.3**	**335.1**	**25.9**	**18.4**	**10.3**	**10.2**
Argentina	84.0	17.6	7.4	3.9	1.6	0.1	0.3	0.9[b]
Barbados	8.1	3.4	-1.0	0.5	3.4	1.8	3.6	0.2[c]
Bolivia	14.5	10.5	9.3	8.5	12.6	7.9	6.7	7.8[b]
Brazil	475	1 149	2 489	929	22.0	9.1	4.3	2.6[b]
Chile	18.7	12.7	12.2	8.9	8.2	6.6	6.0	4.3[b]
Colombia	26.8	25.1	22.6	22.6	19.5	21.6	17.7	16.3[b]
Costa Rica	25.3	17.0	9.0	19.9	22.6	13.9	11.2	12.9[d]
Ecuador	49.0	60.2	31.0	25.4	22.8	25.6	30.6	45.0[b]
El Salvador	9.8	19.9	12.1	8.9	11.4	7.4	1.9	4.3[b]
Guatemala	10.2	14.2	11.6	11.6	8.6	10.9	7.1	7.4[b]
Haiti	6.6	16.1	44.4	32.2	24.8	14.6	15.6	8.2[e]
Honduras	21.4	6.5	13.0	28.9	26.8	25.3	12.7	15.1[b]
Jamaica	80.2	40.2	30.1	26.9	25.5	15.8	9.2	10.2[f]
Mexico	18.8	11.9	8.0	7.1	52.1	27.7	15.7	17.4[b]
Nicaragua	866	3.5	19.5	14.4	11.1	12.1	7.3	17.9[b]
Panama	1.6	1.6	1.0	1.3	0.8	2.3	-0.5	1.5[d]
Paraguay	11.8	17.8	20.4	18.3	10.5	8.2	6.2	16.0[d]
Peru	139	56.7	39.5	15.4	10.2	11.8	6.5	6.0[b]
Dominican Republic	7.9	5.2	2.8	14.3	9.2	4.0	8.4	4.8[d]
Trinidad and Tobago	2.3	8.5	13.4	5.5	3.8	4.3	3.5	6.3[c]
Uruguay	81.3	59.0	52.9	44.1	35.4	24.3	15.2	9.4[b]
Venezuela	31.0	31.9	45.9	70.8	56.6	103.2	37.6	31.2[b]

Source: ECLAC, on the basis of information provided by official sources in the countries.
[a] Figures correspond to the variation in prices during the 12-month period ending in the month indicated.
[b] November 1997-November 1998.
[c] August 1997-August 1998.
[d] October 1997-October 1998.
[e] September 1997-September 1998.
[f] July 1997-July 1998.

Table A-4

LATIN AMERICA AND THE CARIBBEAN: URBAN UNEMPLOYMENT

(Average annual rates)

		1991	1992	1993	1994	1995	1996	1997	1998 [a]
Latin America [b]		**5.8**	**6.1**	**6.2**	**6.3**	**7.2**	**7.7**	**7.3**	**7.9**
Argentina	Urban areas [c]	6.5	7.0	9.6	11.5	17.5	17.2	14.9	12.9 [d]
Barbados [e]	Total national	17.2	23.0	24.3	21.9	19.7	16.4	14.5	12.1 [f]
Bolivia	Departmental capitals	5.8	5.4	5.8	3.1	3.6	3.8	4.4	...
Brazil	Six metropolitan areas	4.8	5.8	5.4	5.1	4.6	5.4	5.7	7.8 [g]
Chile	Total national	8.2	6.7	6.5	7.8	7.4	6.4	6.1	6.1 [g]
Colombia [e]	Seven metropolitan areas	10.2	10.2	8.6	8.9	8.8	11.2	12.4	15.1 [h]
Costa Rica	Total urban	6.0	4.3	4.0	4.3	5.7	6.6	5.9	5.4
Cuba	Total national	7.7	6.1	6.2	6.7	7.9	7.6	6.8	6.5
Ecuador [e]	Total urban	8.5	8.9	8.9	7.8	7.7	10.4	9.3	...
El Salvador	Total urban	7.9	8.2	8.1	7.0	7.0	7.5	7.5	7.2 [i]
Guatemala [j]	Total national	4.0	1.5	2.5	3.3	3.7	3.7	5.0	5.9
Honduras	Total urban	7.4	6.0	7.0	4.0	5.6	6.5	6.4	5.8
Jamaica [e]	Total national	15.4	15.7	16.3	15.4	16.2	16.0	16.5	...
Mexico	Urban areas [c]	2.7	2.8	3.4	3.7	6.2	5.5	3.7	3.3 [g]
Nicaragua [j]	Total national	11.5	14.4	17.8	17.1	16.9	16.0	14.3	12.2
Panama [e]	Metropolitan region	19.3	17.5	15.6	16.0	16.6	16.7	15.4	15.6 [k]
Paraguay	Metropolitan Asunción [l]	5.1	5.3	5.1	4.4	5.3	8.2	7.1	...
Peru	Metropolitan Lima	5.9	9.4	9.9	8.8	8.2	8.0	9.2	9.0 [f]
Dominican Republic [e]	Total national	19.6	20.3	19.9	16.0	15.8	16.5	15.9	14.3
Trinidad and Tobago [e]	Total national	18.5	19.7	19.8	18.4	17.2	16.3	17.2	13.4 [f]
Uruguay	Total urban	8.9	9.0	8.3	9.2	10.3	11.9	11.5	10.0 [m]
Venezuela	Total national	9.5	7.8	6.6	8.7	10.3	11.8	11.4	11.2 [m]

Source: ECLAC, on the basis of official figures.
[a] Preliminary figures.
[b] Does not include the Caribbean countries.
[c] Covers a large and increasing number of urban areas.
[d] Average May, August and October.
[e] Includes hidden unemployment.
[f] First half.
[g] Average January-October.
[h] Average March, June and September.
[i] Average May-October.
[j] Official estimates.
[k] Average March, June and August.
[l] Beginning 1994, figures are for total urban unemployment.
[m] Average January-September.

Table A-5

LATIN AMERICA AND THE CARIBBEAN: AVERAGE REAL WAGES

(Average annual indices: 1990 = 100)

	1991	1992	1993	1994	1995	1996	1997	1998 [a]
Argentina [b]	101.3	102.7	101.3	102.0	100.9	100.7	100.2	99.0 [c]
Bolivia [d]	93.4	97.1	103.6	111.8	112.6	113.8	123.1	...
Brazil [e]	85.2	83.3	91.5	92.2	95.7	103.3	106.0	106.3 [c]
Chile [f]	104.9	109.6	113.5	118.8	123.6	128.7	131.8	135.5 [g]
Colombia [h]	97.4	98.6	103.2	104.1	105.4	107.0	110.0	109.2 [i]
Costa Rica [j]	95.4	99.3	109.5	113.6	111.4	109.1	110.0	...
Mexico [b]	106.5	114.3	124.5	129.1	111.6	99.2	98.6	100.2 [c]
Paraguay [k]	104.7	103.6	104.5	106.1	114.0	117.5	117.0	116.1 [l]
Peru [m]	115.2	111.1	110.2	127.4	116.7	111.2	110.4	108.6 [l]
Uruguay	103.8	106.1	111.2	112.2	109.0	109.7	109.9	112.0 [c]

Source: ECLAC, on the basis of official figures.
[a] Preliminary figures.
[b] Manufacturing.
[c] Estimate based on average January-September.
[d] Private sector in La Paz.
[e] Workers covered by legislation.
[f] Until April 1993, non-agricultural workers; from May 1993 on, general index of hourly wages.
[g] Estimate based on average January-October.
[h] Manual workers in manufacturing.
[i] Average January-August.
[j] Average wages declared by workers covered by social security.
[k] Asunción.
[l] First half.
[m] Private-sector manual workers in the Lima metropolitan area.

Table A-6

LATIN AMERICA AND THE CARIBBEAN: PUBLIC-SECTOR DEFICIT (-) OR SURPLUS [a]

(Percentages of GDP)

Country	Coverage	1991	1992	1993	1994	1995	1996	1997	1998[b]
Argentina	NNFPS	-1.6	-0.1	1.4	-0.2	-0.6	-1.8	-1.4	-1.2
Bolivia	NFPS	-4.3	-4.4	-6.1	-3.0	-1.8	-2.0	-3.4	-4.1
Brazil	NFPS [c]	...	...	...	...	-7.4	-5.9	-6.2	-7.0
Brazil	NFPS [d]	-0.2	-1.8	-0.8	1.1	-4.9	-3.9	-4.4	-6.8
Chile	CG	1.5	2.3	2.0	1.7	2.6	2.3	1.9	0.7
Colombia	NFPS	0.0	-0.1	0.3	2.6	-0.5	-2.0	-3.6	-3.4
Costa Rica	CG	-3.1	-1.9	-1.9	-6.9	-4.4	-5.2	-4.0	-2.9
Ecuador	NFPS	-1.0	-1.7	-0.4	-0.2	-1.5	-3.1	-2.5	-6.0
El Salvador	CG	-3.2	-2.1	-1.5	-0.8	-0.5	-2.0	-1.1	-1.6
Guatemala	CG	-0.1	-0.5	-1.5	-1.4	-0.7	-0.1	-1.1	-1.6
Haiti	CG	-0.3	-4.4	-3.3	-3.3	-4.8	-1.6	-2.0	-1.2
Honduras	CG	-3.3	-4.9	-9.9	-7.0	-4.2	-3.8	-2.8	-3.5
Mexico	NFPS	-0.4	1.6	0.7	-0.3	-0.2	-0.1	-0.4	-1.4
Nicaragua	CG	4.1	-3.4	0.0	-5.1	-0.5	-1.5	-1.5	-0.1
Panama	CG	-2.5	-1.3	0.5	-0.7	0.7	-1.7	-0.6	-4.0
Paraguay	CG	0.8	-1.4	-0.7	1.0	-0.3	-0.8	-0.2	-1.5
Peru	NFPS [e]	-0.9	-1.5	-1.2	3.0	-0.1	-1.0	0.0	-0.1
Dominican Republic	CG	3.2	3.6	0.2	-0.8	0.6	-0.4	0.8	-0.6
Uruguay	NFPS	1.3	1.5	-0.8	-2.5	-1.3	-1.2	-1.3	-1.2
Venezuela	NFPS	-2.2	-5.9	-1.3	-13.8	-6.9	7.6	2.3	-5.7
Average		**-0.6**	**-1.4**	**-1.3**	**-1.9**	**-1.7**	**-1.3**	**-1.4**	**-2.4**

Source: ECLAC, on the basis of official figures.

Note: Abbreviations used: CG = Central government. NFPS = Non-financial public sector. NNFPS = National non-financial public sector (does not include provinces or municipalities).

[a] Calculated on the basis of figures in local currency at current prices.
[b] Preliminary estimates.
[c] Refers to the nominal financial balance.
[d] Refers to the operational financial balance.
[e] To 1995, includes privatization proceeds.

Table A-7

LATIN AMERICA AND THE CARIBBEAN: INDICES OF THE REAL EFFECTIVE EXCHANGE RATE FOR IMPORTS [a]

(Indices: 1995 = 100)

	1991	1992	1993	1994	1995	1996	1997	1998[b]
Argentina	116.3	103.0	94.4	93.8	100.0	101.9	98.9	96.4
Barbados	92.6	93.2	95.0	98.3	100.0	99.4	93.6	95.2
Bolivia	83.8	87.6	92.7	97.7	100.0	93.4	91.1	86.8
Brazil	108.5	116.4	112.6	113.6	100.0	94.2	93.2	95.5
Chile	111.8	107.9	110.1	106.3	100.0	96.4	90.0	92.0
Colombia	134.9	119.5	114.5	99.9	100.0	92.7	86.8	90.0
Costa Rica	108.3	103.2	103.1	103.6	100.0	99.0	101.2	101.9
Ecuador	114.8	116.1	103.4	98.1	100.0	100.4	96.2	92.5
El Salvador	125.4	124.8	112.5	105.7	100.0	92.2	91.9	91.1
Guatemala	110.0	108.3	110.2	104.6	100.0	95.2	90.4	90.4
Haiti	116.3	118.7	141.3	113.4	100.0	85.0	73.0	67.6
Honduras	98.1	92.8	103.9	115.4	100.0	101.6	96.2	88.6
Jamaica	92.8	107.9	101.1	103.6	100.0	84.2	72.3	68.0
Mexico	74.8	69.0	65.8	67.6	100.0	89.0	77.2	76.1
Nicaragua	84.7	85.5	89.7	95.4	100.0	102.2	107.0	109.1
Paraguay	96.5	102.6	106.4	100.5	100.0	95.7	94.0	104.2
Peru	94.8	95.5	106.2	100.2	100.0	98.6	99.1	98.7
Dominican Republic	104.5	107.1	106.5	103.0	100.0	93.5	95.7	102.7
Trinidad and Tobago	75.3	76.6	89.9	97.0	100.0	98.7	99.6	95.1
Uruguay	130.2	127.5	113.9	104.3	100.0	99.1	97.1	96.5
Venezuela	130.6	124.7	121.3	126.4	100.0	119.2	92.6	77.2

Source: ECLAC, on the basis of figures provided by the International Monetary Fund.

[a] The average of the indices for the real (main official) exchange rate for the currency of each country against the currencies of its main trading partners, weighted according to the relative magnitude of imports from those countries. The weightings reflect the average for 1992-1996. Consumer price indices were used in the calculations for each country. For information on the methodology and sources used, see ECLAC, *Economic Survey of Latin America, 1981* (E/CEPAL/G.1248), Santiago, Chile, 1983. United Nations publication, Sales No. E.83.II.G.2.

[b] Average January-September.

Table A-8

LATIN AMERICA AND THE CARIBBEAN: EXPORTS OF GOODS, FOB

(Indices: 1995 = 100)

	Value			Unit value			Volume		
	1996	1997	1998[a]	1996	1997	1998[a]	1996	1997	1998[a]
Latin America and the Caribbean	**111.8**	**124.6**	**122.8**	**99.5**	**97.2**	**88.9**	**112.4**	**128.1**	**138.1**
Argentina	113.6	125.1	125.5	102.0	96.3	87.8	111.4	129.9	142.8
Bolivia	108.7	112.1	106.6	83.9	83.0	75.3	129.6	135.1	141.6
Brazil	102.7	113.9	109.7	99.3	100.8	94.8	103.4	113.0	115.7
Chile	96.1	105.6	94.2	83.7	83.0	71.4	114.9	127.2	132.0
Colombia	104.2	114.3	110.8	100.6	103.9	93.5	103.6	110.0	118.5
Costa Rica	108.1	123.6	153.2	94.6	98.3	96.6	114.3	125.8	158.5
Ecuador	111.1	119.3	101.8	108.1	109.7	95.4	102.8	108.8	106.7
El Salvador	107.7	145.4	148.8	85.9	93.0	91.1	125.4	156.3	163.2
Guatemala	103.5	120.4	131.0	71.0	82.4	82.0	145.7	146.2	159.7
Haiti	107.8	140.6	156.6	96.0	101.8	97.7	112.3	138.1	160.3
Honduras	111.3	126.0	137.6	83.4	99.5	99.9	133.5	126.6	137.8
Mexico	120.7	138.8	147.3	100.6	94.4	89.0	120.0	147.1	165.5
Nicaragua	127.5	133.7	115.9	93.2	85.3	85.1	136.8	156.8	136.2
Panama	95.9	110.3	108.6	98.1	100.1	93.4	97.8	110.2	116.3
Paraguay	94.6	85.3	80.0	110.2	127.1	114.4	85.9	67.1	70.0
Peru	105.5	121.9	100.5	97.8	103.2	88.8	107.9	118.1	113.3
Dominican Republic	114.8	131.5	134.7	99.2	100.5	94.3	115.8	130.8	142.8
Uruguay	114.0	129.5	135.3	94.8	92.4	91.5	120.3	140.1	147.9
Venezuela	124.2	124.2	92.8	112.5	108.8	81.1	110.4	114.2	114.5

Source: ECLAC, on the basis of figures provided by the International Monetary Fund and national agencies.
[a] Preliminary figures.

Table A-9

LATIN AMERICA AND THE CARIBBEAN: IMPORTS OF GOODS, FOB

(Indices: 1995 = 100)

	Value			Unit value			Volume		
	1996	1997	1998[a]	1996	1997	1998[a]	1996	1997	1998[a]
Latin America and the Caribbean	**110.8**	**131.8**	**139.1**	**100.4**	**94.5**	**90.2**	**110.3**	**139.4**	**154.3**
Argentina	118.5	152.1	160.7	97.7	90.3	86.2	121.3	168.5	186.4
Bolivia	111.8	134.2	144.6	98.5	94.2	89.5	113.5	142.4	161.6
Brazil	106.9	123.1	113.3	108.0	103.6	97.4	99.0	118.8	116.4
Chile	112.6	124.3	124.2	100.3	95.8	92.1	112.3	129.8	134.9
Colombia	99.0	111.5	114.8	96.9	89.6	86.0	102.2	124.5	133.5
Costa Rica	105.4	123.8	147.7	99.7	97.7	92.4	105.7	126.7	159.8
Ecuador	90.7	115.0	128.2	98.6	98.0	93.1	92.0	117.4	137.7
El Salvador	93.8	110.6	129.3	100.4	94.1	90.0	93.4	117.5	143.7
Guatemala	95.0	116.8	140.1	101.8	93.5	88.4	93.3	125.0	158.6
Haiti	96.5	99.2	92.8	102.8	100.7	94.0	93.9	98.5	98.7
Honduras	112.0	131.1	154.7	95.7	88.4	82.5	117.0	148.3	187.5
Mexico	123.5	151.6	172.0	97.9	91.9	89.0	126.1	164.9	193.2
Nicaragua	121.6	158.5	160.7	101.4	98.6	92.5	119.9	160.7	173.7
Panama	97.1	110.3	113.8	98.0	90.5	86.0	99.0	121.9	132.3
Paraguay	97.5	93.8	81.5	99.7	95.2	90.0	97.8	98.5	90.5
Peru	101.6	110.2	107.4	101.3	91.4	86.2	100.3	120.6	124.6
Dominican Republic	111.3	128.4	147.0	103.2	100.1	93.1	107.9	128.3	157.9
Uruguay	115.7	129.3	133.7	101.0	99.6	94.0	114.5	129.8	142.2
Venezuela	82.3	107.2	114.5	97.3	90.9	87.7	84.6	117.9	130.5

Source: ECLAC, on the basis of figures provided by the International Monetary Fund and national agencies.
[a] Preliminary figures.

Table A-10

LATIN AMERICA AND THE CARIBBEAN: TERMS OF TRADE (GOODS), FOB/FOB

(Indices: 1995 = 100)

	1991	1992	1993	1994	1995	1996	1997	1998[a]
Latin America and the Caribbean	**99.2**	**95.8**	**94.8**	**96.8**	**100.0**	**99.1**	**102.8**	**98.6**
Argentina	104.0	102.6	108.6	106.1	100.0	104.4	106.6	101.8
Bolivia	115.8	94.7	88.3	102.5	100.0	85.2	88.1	84.1
Brazil	87.2	81.4	83.9	87.0	100.0	91.9	97.3	97.3
Chile	83.2	82.1	75.3	87.1	100.0	83.4	86.6	77.5
Colombia	99.8	81.8	84.8	97.6	100.0	103.8	116.0	108.7
Costa Rica	79.8	81.0	84.5	93.9	100.0	94.9	100.6	104.5
Ecuador	122.2	113.9	106.2	108.9	100.0	109.6	111.9	102.5
El Salvador	70.6	61.1	63.7	81.0	100.0	85.6	98.8	101.3
Guatemala	84.2	83.8	87.6	94.9	100.0	69.7	88.1	92.8
Haiti	97.8	92.9	94.1	96.8	100.0	93.4	101.1	103.9
Honduras	88.4	83.8	91.9	92.1	100.0	87.1	112.6	121.1
Mexico	105.6	102.7	103.4	101.3	100.0	102.8	102.7	100.0
Nicaragua	99.2	72.6	82.0	96.4	100.0	91.9	86.5	92.0
Panama	82.2	104.0	106.8	110.1	100.0	100.1	110.6	108.6
Paraguay	86.7	79.4	87.2	105.1	100.0	110.5	133.5	127.1
Peru	81.9	92.1	88.9	80.7	100.0	96.5	112.9	103.0
Dominican Republic	94.7	88.5	86.9	91.5	100.0	96.1	100.4	101.3
Uruguay	98.3	103.3	96.8	91.2	100.0	93.9	92.8	97.3
Venezuela	125.2	119.9	110.7	103.1	100.0	115.6	119.7	92.4

Source: ECLAC.
[a] Preliminary figures.

Table A-11

LATIN AMERICA AND THE CARIBBEAN: BALANCE OF PAYMENTS

(Millions of dollars)

	Exports of goods (f.o.b.) and services			Imports of goods (f.o.b.) and services			Balance on goods			Balance on services		
	1996	1997	1998[a]	1996	1997	1998[a]	1996	1997	1998[a]	1996	1997	1998[a]
Latin America and the Caribbean	**296 473**	**327 376**	**327 310**	**304 432**	**359 026**	**377 715**	**5 982**	**-12 295**	**-32 910**	**-13 941**	**-19 355**	**-17 495**
Argentina	27 037	29 318	29 450	27 910	34 899	36 650	1 622	-2 272	-3 800	-2 495	-3 309	-3 400
Bolivia	1 313	1 362	1 310	1 731	2 048	2 145	-236	-475	-660	-182	-211	-175
Brazil	54 524	60 252	60 000	69 110	79 821	76 750	-5 539	-8 372	-5 500	-9 047	-11 197	-11 250
Chile	18 771	20 608	18 940	20 219	22 219	22 445	-1 095	-1 295	-3 100	-353	-316	-405
Colombia	14 590	15 888	15 765	16 746	18 756	19 135	-2 143	-2 727	-3 505	-13	-141	135
Costa Rica	4 861	5 472	6 600	5 036	5 723	6 765	-224	-380	-260	49	129	95
Ecuador	5 748	6 000	5 240	4 548	5 787	6 325	1 220	598	-710	-20	-385	-375
El Salvador	2 203	2 706	2 740	3 466	3 885	4 340	-1 198	-1 107	-1 645	-65	-72	45
Guatemala	2 767	3 175	3 685	3 534	4 187	4 980	-648	-945	-1 425	-119	-67	130
Haiti	257	289	300	782	801	720	-351	-320	-265	-174	-192	-155
Honduras	1 911	2 187	2 385	2 118	2 472	2 880	-133	-220	-420	-74	-65	-75
Mexico	106 901	121 701	129 200	100 060	122 109	137 400	6 531	623	-7 400	310	-1 031	-800
Nicaragua	807	867	800	1 300	1 608	1 645	-381	-667	-780	-112	-74	-65
Panama	7 510	8 440	8 540	7 501	8 605	8 965	-629	-636	-970	638	471	545
Paraguay	4 547	4 184	3 895	5 022	4 960	4 280	-379	-606	-275	-97	-170	-110
Peru	7 312	8 354	7 415	9 985	10 840	10 690	-1 988	-1 738	-2 715	-685	-748	-560
Dominican Republic	6 287	7 197	7 510	6 611	7 574	8 440	-1 532	-1 806	-2 645	1 208	1 429	1 715
Uruguay	3 847	4 256	4 310	3 974	4 450	4 590	-686	-723	-720	559	529	440
Venezuela	25 280	25 120	19 225	14 779	18 282	18 570	13 770	10 773	3 885	-3 269	-3 935	-3 230

Table A-11 (continued)

	Trade balance			Current transfers			Balance on the income account			Balance on the current account		
	1996	1997	1998[a]	1996	1997	1998[a]	1996	1997	1998[a]	1996	1997	1998[a]
Latin America and the Caribbean	**-7 959**	**-31 650**	**-50 405**	**14 395**	**14 807**	**16 315**	**-43 095**	**-46 826**	**-49 815**	**-36 659**	**-63 669**	**-83 905**
Argentina	-873	-5 581	-7 200	334	346	300	-3 248	-4 219	-5 300	-3 787	-9 454	-12 200
Bolivia	-418	-686	-835	222	238	265	-208	-266	-235	-404	-714	-805
Brazil	-14 586	-19 569	-16 750	2 899	2 176	2 000	-12 660	-16 091	-17 700	-24 347	-33 484	-32 450
Chile	-1 448	-1 611	-3 505	500	528	455	-2 796	-2 975	-2 110	-3 744	-4 058	-5 160
Colombia	-2 156	-2 868	-3 370	532	611	575	-3 322	-3 426	-3 265	-4 946	-5 683	-6 060
Costa Rica	-175	-251	-165	150	114	105	-84	-192	-315	-109	-329	-375
Ecuador	1 200	213	-1 085	290	391	730	-1 379	-1 350	-1 410	111	-746	-1 765
El Salvador	-1 263	-1 179	-1 600	1 254	1 363	1 395	-90	-87	-30	-99	97	-235
Guatemala	-767	-1 012	-1 295	587	691	735	-211	-226	-140	-391	-547	-700
Haiti	-525	-512	-420	463	449	320	-11	-14	-10	-73	-77	-110
Honduras	-207	-285	-495	277	312	410	-258	-218	-210	-188	-191	-295
Mexico	6 841	-408	-8 200	4 531	5 247	6 200	-13 702	-12 288	-13 500	-2 330	-7 449	-15 500
Nicaragua	-493	-741	-845	95	150	200	-300	-222	-160	-698	-813	-805
Panama	9	-165	-425	149	160	160	-317	-304	-330	-159	-309	-595
Paraguay	-475	-776	-385	55	47	60	103	87	90	-317	-642	-235
Peru	-2 673	-2 486	-3 275	689	681	680	-1 635	-1 603	-1 525	-3 619	-3 408	-4 120
Dominican Republic	-324	-377	-930	1 147	1 345	1 720	-1 063	-1 193	-1 295	-240	-225	-505
Uruguay	-127	-194	-280	83	81	70	-189	-208	-220	-233	-321	-430
Venezuela	10 501	6 838	655	138	-123	-65	-1 725	-2 031	-2 150	8 914	4 684	-1 560

Table A-11 (concluded)

	Balance on the capital and financial account [b]			Overall balance			Reserve assets [c] (variation)			IMF loans and credit and exceptional financing		
	1996	1997	1998[a]	1996	1997	1998[a]	1996	1997	1998[a]	1996	1997	1998[a]
Latin America and the Caribbean	**62 432**	**80 431**	**62 320**	**25 773**	**16 762**	**-21 585**	**-25 617**	**-15 786**	**15 050**	**-156**	**-976**	**6 535**
Argentina	7 025	12 516	15 200	3 238	3 062	3 000	-3 775	-3 062	-3 000	537	0	0
Bolivia	672	807	720	268	93	-85	-310	-90	85	42	-3	0
Brazil	33 121	25 647	17 450	8 774	-7 837	-15 000	-8 664	7 871	10 000	-110	-34	5 000
Chile	6 249	7 243	2 460	2 505	3 185	-2 700	-1 108	-3 185	2 700	-1 397	0	0
Colombia	6 428	5 653	4 635	1 482	-30	-1 425	-1 482	30	1 425	0	0	0
Costa Rica	54	545	295	-55	216	-80	55	-216	80	0	0	0
Ecuador	-252	779	725	-141	33	-1 040	-245	-237	245	386	204	795
El Salvador	264	267	635	165	364	400	-165	-364	-400	0	0	0
Guatemala	567	834	900	176	287	200	-176	-287	-200	0	0	0
Haiti	24	117	105	-49	40	-5	49	-51	15	0	11	-10
Honduras	294	404	230	106	213	-65	-175	-296	0	69	83	65
Mexico	4 104	17 959	16 500	1 774	10 510	1 000	-986	-10 510	-1 000	-788	0	0
Nicaragua	215	820	640	-483	7	-165	-79	-174	-45	562	167	210
Panama	442	786	1 195	283	477	600	-318	-746	-600	35	269	0
Paraguay	289	444	105	-28	-198	-130	44	216	145	-16	-18	-15
Peru	4 579	5 865	3 045	960	2 457	-1 075	-1 882	-1 628	700	922	-829	375
Dominican Republic	201	458	500	-39	233	-5	15	-40	-110	24	-193	115
Uruguay	386	721	580	153	400	150	-141	-392	-150	-12	-8	0
Venezuela	-2 230	-1 434	-3 600	6 684	3 250	-5 160	-6 274	-2 625	5 160	-410	-625	0

Source: ECLAC, on the basis of figures provided by the International Monetary Fund and national agencies.
[a] Preliminary estimates. Figures have been rounded to the nearest five or ten.
[b] Includes errors and omissions.
[c] A minus sign (-) indicates and increase in reserve assets.

Table A-12

LATIN AMERICA AND THE CARIBBEAN: NET FOREIGN DIRECT INVESTMENT [a][b]

(Millions of dollars)

	1991	1992	1993	1994	1995	1996	1997	1998[c]
Latin America and the Caribbean	**10 955**	**13 262**	**11 555**	**24 471**	**26 958**	**37 584**	**57 131**	**53 195**
Argentina	2 439	4 019	3 262	2 982	4 628	4 885	6 647	5 800
Bolivia	50	91	121	147	391	472	599	650
Brazil	89	1 924	801	2 035	3 475	9 123	18 601	22 500
Chile	697	538	600	1 672	2 220	3 561	3 467	2 500
Colombia	433	679	719	1 501	1 943	3 208	5 192	2 625
Costa Rica	172	222	244	293	390	422	482	520
Ecuador	160	178	469	531	470	447	577	750
El Salvador	25	15	16	...	38	-7	...	875[d]
Guatemala	91	94	143	65	75	77	85	600
Haiti	14	-2	-2	-3	7	4	5	5
Honduras	52	48	52	42	69	90	128	100
Mexico	4 742	4 393	4 389	10 973	9 526	9 189	12 748	9 300
Nicaragua	...	15	39	40	70	85	173	185
Panama	41	139	156	374	220	369	1 000	675
Paraguay	84	120	74	97	156	246	221	245
Peru	-7	136	670	3 083	2 048	3 242	2 030	2 070
Dominican Republic	145	180	214	348	389	358	405	495
Uruguay	...	...	102	155	157	137	160	155
Venezuela	1 728	473	-514	136	686	1 676	4 611	3 145

Source: ECLAC, on the basis of balance-of-payments figures provided by the International Monetary Fund and national agencies.

[a] Refers to direct investment in the reporting economy minus direct investment abroad by residents. For some countries this information is not available. Includes reinvested earnings.

[b] In accordance with the fifth edition of the *IMF Balance of Payments Manual*, all transactions between non-financial direct investment enterprises and their parent companies and affiliates are included in direct investment.

[c] Preliminary figures.

[d] Beginning 1998, the Central Reserve Bank of El Salvador systematically records foreign direct investment.

Table A-13

LATIN AMERICA AND THE CARIBBEAN: INTERNATIONAL BOND ISSUES [a]

(Millions of dollars)

	1991	1992	1993	1994	1995	1996	1997	1998[b]
Latin America and the Caribbean	7 242	12 577	28 794	18 241	23 395	47 157	54 365	33 667
Argentina	795	1 570	6 308	5 319	6 354	13 738	14 790	12 887
Bahamas	-	-	-	50	-	-	-	250
Bolivia	-	-	-	10	-	-	-	
Brazil	1 837	3 655	3 655	3 998	7 041	11 194	14 722	7 997
Chile	200	120	120	155	300	1 750	1 700	650
Colombia	-	-	-	955	1 083	1 751	1 000	1 389
Ecuador	-	-	-	-	10	-	625	-
Guatemala	-	-	-	-	-	-	150	-
Jamaica	-	-	-	55	-	-	200	250
Mexico	3 782	6 100	6 100	6 949	7 646	17 823	13 767	6 244
Panama	50	-	-	250	324	75	1 315	300
Dominican Republic	-	-	-	-	-	-	200	-
Trinidad and Tobago	-	100	100	150	71	150	-	-
Uruguay	-	100	100	200	211	145	479	350
Venezuela	578	932	932	-	356	532	5 415	3 150

Source: International Monetary Fund, Research Department, Emerging Markets Studies Division.
[a] Gross issues. Includes medium-term euronotes.
[b] January-October 1998.

Table A-14

LATIN AMERICA AND THE CARIBBEAN: INDICES OF STOCK EXCHANGE PRICES IN DOLLARS [a]

(Indices: June 1997 = 100)

	1991	1992	1993	1994	1995	1996	1997	1998	
								June	December[b]
Latin America	**49.0**	**51.0**	**77.4**	**76.2**	**62.5**	**72.5**	**90.6**	**72.0**	**53.9**
Argentina	70.0	50.7	84.9	63.6	69.1	82.1	96.3	78.7	64.9
Brazil	20.2	20.0	38.2	64.0	49.8	64.9	78.3	67.4	43.0
Chile	46.7	52.4	67.8	95.8	93.0	77.0	79.6	62.5	54.1
Colombia	45.5	62.0	81.6	103.5	77.1	80.5	99.9	69.0	53.2
Mexico	88.5	106.2	156.0	91.1	66.5	77.3	114.1	86.1	67.7
Peru	-	32.6	43.9	66.8	73.1	73.6	83.8	73.7	51.1
Venezuela	128.0	73.3	65.6	47.8	32.7	75.7	93.3	46.8	41.6

Source: ECLAC, on the basis of figures provided by the International Finance Corporation.
[a] Figures at end of month, general index.
[b] As of December 14.

Table A-15

LATIN AMERICA AND THE CARIBBEAN: TOTAL DISBURSED EXTERNAL DEBT [a]

(Millions of dollars)

	1991	1992	1993	1994	1995	1996	1997	1998 [b]
Latin America and the Caribbean	**452 388**	**469 001**	**523 099**	**556 730**	**606 188**	**627 026**	**649 998**	**697 797**
Argentina [c]	58 413	59 123	67 802	79 069	89 321	99 500	110 200	118 200
Bolivia [d]	3 582	3 784	3 777	4 216	4 523	4 366	4 232	4 250
Brazil [e]	123 811	135 949	145 726	148 295	159 256	178 161	200 000	222 500
Chile	17 319	18 965	19 665	21 968	21 736	22 979	26 701	30 670
Colombia	17 335	17 277	18 942	21 954	25 050	29 471	31 806	34 000
Costa Rica	3 992	3 992	3 827	3 818	3 888	3 376	3 305	3 430
Cuba	...	...	8 785	9 083	10 504	10 465	10 146	10 200
Ecuador	12 802	12 795	13 631	14 589	13 934	14 586	15 099	16 100
El Salvador [d]	2 102	2 338	1 988	2 069	2 343	2 517	2 667	2 690
Guatemala [d]	2 403	2 252	2 086	2 160	2 107	2 075	2 131	2 400
Guyana	1 873	2 054	2 062	2 004	2 058	1 537	1 514	1 550
Haiti [d]	809	873	866	875	898	914	1 025	1 100
Honduras	3 441	3 589	3 850	4 040	4 243	4 123	4 095	4 150
Jamaica	3 874	3 678	3 687	3 652	3 452	3 232	3 278	3 300
Mexico [f]	117 000	116 501	130 524	139 818	164 200	157 200	149 700	158 000
Nicaragua [d]	10 316	10 414	11 887	11 695	10 299	6 094	6 001	6 280
Panama [d]	3 699	3 548	3 494	3 663	3 938	5 069	5 051	5 350
Paraguay	1 637	1 249	1 218	1 241	1 328	1 336	1 438	1 620
Peru	20 787	21 409	27 489	30 392	33 515	33 805	28 508	29 780
Dominican Republic [d]	4 614	4 413	4 562	3 946	3 999	3 796	3 502	3 470
Trinidad and Tobago	2 438	2 215	2 102	2 064	1 905	1 876	1 527	1 407
Uruguay [d]	4 141	4 136	4 293	4 959	5 193	5 367	5 618	5 750
Venezuela	36 000	38 447	40 836	41 160	38 498	35 181	32 454	31 600

Source: ECLAC, on the basis of official figures.

[a] Includes debt owed to the International Monetary Fund.

[b] Preliminary figures.

[c] The figures refer only to the stock of gross public-sector debt and some categories of private-sector debt. They do not include private-sector short-term financial debt, nor, since the category is gross debt, do they reflect the stock of private-sector assets abroad.

[d] Public external debt.

[e] The increase in external debt is in gross terms. In 1998 there was a short-term outflow equal to some US$ 25 billion, part of which corresponded to payments on private external debt and to acquisitions of assets abroad by Brazilians. These items have not yet been determined.

[f] Does not include investment by non-residents in government securities.

Table A-16

LATIN AMERICA AND THE CARIBBEAN: NET RESOURCE TRANSFERS [a]

(Millions of dollars)

	1991	1992	1993	1994	1995	1996	1997	1998 [b]
Latin America and the Caribbean	**4 317**	**25 880**	**30 946**	**8 211**	**17 560**	**19 181**	**32 629**	**19 040**
Argentina	-1 573	6 152	9 257	7 399	-497	4 314	8 297	9 900
Bolivia	24	377	200	45	250	506	538	485
Brazil	-8 570	584	-1 633	-723	19 759	20 351	9 522	4 750
Chile	-780	1 422	1 070	2 004	-589	2 056	4 268	350
Colombia	-2 303	-1 561	732	1 179	1 960	3 106	2 227	1 370
Costa Rica	341	319	393	238	300	-30	353	-20
Ecuador	-557	-1 055	-132	-151	-761	-1 245	-367	110
El Salvador	22	190	118	36	383	174	180	605
Guatemala	632	513	704	611	210	356	608	760
Haiti	12	37	63	-6	184	13	114	85
Honduras	35	108	-4	151	51	105	269	85
Mexico	14 777	16 406	18 427	-1 099	-1 687	-10 386	5 671	3 000
Nicaragua	212	340	136	345	352	477	765	690
Panama	-23	-236	-75	-135	-17	160	751	865
Paraguay	617	-495	-108	519	500	376	513	180
Peru	979	1 164	1 411	3 894	3 225	3 866	3 433	1 895
Dominican Republic	322	449	22	-781	-428	-838	-928	-680
Uruguay	-161	8	231	295	204	185	505	360
Venezuela	311	1 158	134	-5 610	-5 839	-4 365	-4 090	-5 750

Source: ECLAC, on the basis of figures provided by the International Monetary Fund and national agencies.

[a] The net transfer of resources is equal to net capital inflows (including non- autonomous inflows and errors and omissions) minus the balance on the income account (net payments of profits and interest). Negative figures indicate net outward resource transfers.

[b] Preliminary figures.

Table A-17

LATIN AMERICA AND THE CARIBBEAN: RATIO OF TOTAL ACCRUED INTEREST
TO EXPORTS OF GOODS AND SERVICES [a]

(Percentages)

	1991	1992	1993	1994	1995	1996	1997	1998[b]
Latin America and the Caribbean	**21.7**	**18.7**	**18.1**	**16.6**	**16.6**	**15.2**	**14.5**	**15.5**
Argentina	36.1	23.3	22.0	24.6	24.0	23.2	24.3	26.1
Bolivia	29.2	24.3	21.2	14.3	16.6	15.8	15.6	16.8
Brazil	27.2	20.8	21.8	17.9	20.5	23.4	23.9	25.7
Chile	14.7	11.4	10.3	8.2	7.3	7.0	6.7	7.7
Colombia	16.4	14.6	12.3	12.9	13.6	14.5	14.8	16.7
Costa Rica	10.1	7.3	6.6	5.5	5.7	2.7	3.9	4.2
Ecuador	31.3	24.1	23.2	20.7	17.2	17.6	16.5	19.8
El Salvador	12.6	10.5	10.3	6.3	5.6	6.1	6.0	5.3
Guatemala	7.1	8.9	6.2	5.8	4.7	6.1	5.2	3.5
Haiti	7.6	5.4	8.4	6.9	11.2	3.9	4.2	3.3
Honduras	21.1	25.9	15.5	15.6	13.1	11.4	8.9	8.0
Mexico	18.0	17.5	18.3	16.7	15.5	12.7	10.5	10.5
Nicaragua	110.4	158.6	115.8	102.2	54.5	35.7	24.7	19.4
Panama	22.9	19.1	15.7	15.4	21.8	16.3	15.0	15.2
Paraguay	4.7	8.5	3.1	2.0	2.7	2.1	2.3	2.5
Peru	36.7	37.3	38.9	34.5	33.2	25.0	19.6	25.2
Dominican Republic	8.6	9.1	6.0	4.8	4.9	3.8	3.1	3.1
Uruguay	21.2	15.7	14.4	14.9	18.0	15.1	16.8	16.6
Venezuela	15.4	18.3	17.0	17.0	16.1	11.2	13.6	18.3

Source: ECLAC, on the basis of figures provided by the International Monetary Fund and national agencies.
[a] Includes interest paid and interest due and not paid.
[b] Preliminary figures.

Table A-18

**LATIN AMERICA AND THE CARIBBEAN: RATIO OF PROFIT PAYMENTS
TO EXPORTS OF GOODS AND SERVICES** [a]

(Percentages)

	1991	1992	1993	1994	1995	1996	1997	1998 [b]
Latin America and the Caribbean	**4.2**	**4.5**	**5.2**	**5.8**	**5.5**	**5.7**	**6.6**	**7.5**
Argentina	5.6	7.7	10.8	9.9	7.9	6.1	8.6	10.9
Bolivia	0.4	2.6	1.9	2.2	3.1	1.0	6.5	5.7
Brazil	3.0	2.1	4.5	4.7	7.5	7.0	11.1	10.5
Chile	7.9	8.4	8.1	12.9	11.4	11.9	12.7	9.3
Colombia	7.9	10.2	10.3	10.6	12.5	14.2	13.3	11.6
Costa Rica	3.0	3.0	2.9	1.7	2.4	1.8	2.9	2.4
Ecuador	3.8	3.5	4.0	3.9	3.7	3.4	3.3	3.6
El Salvador	4.0	2.7	2.2	1.6	1.3	...	...	...
Guatemala	2.6	1.9	2.6	2.6	2.6	3.7	4.4	2.8
Haiti	2.6	...	...	...	1.7	...	0.7	...
Honduras	7.1	7.1	4.5	1.8	3.6	3.7	2.7	2.9
Mexico	4.8	4.2	4.1	5.3	3.2	3.9	3.4	3.8
Nicaragua	4.2	5.1	4.8	3.8	4.0	6.4	5.0	5.1
Panama	...	3.9	2.7	2.2	2.3	2.7	2.7	3.1
Paraguay	1.0	1.2	1.5	1.0	1.3	1.5	0.9	1.1
Peru	0.9	3.5	3.0	3.3	5.2	5.7	8.3	6.1
Dominican Republic	6.5	10.6	7.7	9.1	8.8	14.8	15.0	15.6
Uruguay	...	...	1.7	1.3	...	...	0.9	1.0
Venezuela	1.4	3.3	3.6	2.9	2.1	1.7	2.4	1.8

Source: ECLAC, on the basis of figures provided by the International Monetary Fund and national agencies.
[a] Includes reinvested profits.
[b] Preliminary figures.

ECLAC
publications

ECONOMIC COMMISSION FOR LATIN AMERICA AND THE
CARIBBEAN
Casilla 179-D Santiago, Chile

PERIODIC PUBLICATIONS

CEPAL Review

CEPAL Review first appeared in 1976 as part of the Publications Programme of the Economic Commission for Latin America and the Caribbean, its aim being to make a contribution to the study of the economic and social development problems of the region. The views expressed in signed articles, including those by Secretariat staff members, are those of the authors and therefore do not necessarily reflect the point of view of the Organization.

CEPAL Review is published in Spanish and English versions three times a year.

Annual subscription costs for 1999 are US$ 30 for the Spanish version and US$ 35 for the English version. The price of single issues is US$ 15 in both cases.

The cost of a two-year subscription (1999-2000) is US$ 50 for Spanish-language version and US$ 60 for English.

Revista de la CEPAL, número extraordinario: CEPAL CINCUENTA AÑOS, reflexiones sobre América Latina y el Caribe, 1998, 376 pp.

Panorama Económico de América Latina, 1996, 83 pp.

Economic Panorama of Latin America, 1996, 83 pp.

Síntesis estudio económico de América Latina y el Caribe, 1997-1998, 1998, 34 pp.

Summary Economic Survey of Latin America and the Caribbean 1997-1998, 1998, 34 pp.

Balance Preliminar de la Economía de América Latina y el Caribe, 1997, 64 pp.

Preliminary Overview of Economy of Latin America and the Caribbean, 1997, 60 pp.

Panorama Social de América Latina, 1997, 232 pp.

Social Panorama of Latin America, 1997, 232 pp.

La Inversión Extranjera en América Latina y el Caribe, 1998, 290 pp.

Estudio Económico de América Latina y el Caribe		*Economic Survey of Latin America and the Caribbean*	
1994-1995,	348 pp.	***1994-1995,***	332 pp.
1995-1996,	349 pp.	***1995-1996,***	335 pp.
1996-1997,	354 pp.	***1996-1997,***	335 pp.
1997-1998,	386 pp.	***1997-1998,***	360 pp.

(Issues for previous years also available)

Anuario Estadístico de América Latina y el Caribe / **Statistical Yearbook for Latin America and the Caribbean** (bilingual)

1989,	770 pp.	*1994,*	863 pp.
1990,	782 pp.	*1995,*	865 pp.
1991,	856 pp.	*1996,*	866 pp.
1992,	868 pp.	*1997,*	894 pp.
1993,	860 pp.		

(Issues for previous years also available)

Libros de la C E P A L

1 *Manual de proyectos de desarrollo económico*, 1958, 5th. ed. 1980, 264 pp.

1 ***Manual on economic development projects,*** 1958, 2nd. ed. 1972, 242 pp. (Out of stock)

2 *América Latina en el umbral de los años ochenta*, 1979, 2nd. ed. 1980, 203 pp.

3 *Agua, desarrollo y medio ambiente en América Latina*, 1980, 443 pp.

4 *Los bancos transnacionales y el financiamiento externo de América Latina. La experiencia del Perú*, 1980, 265 pp.

4 ***Transnational banks and the external finance of Latin America: the experience of Peru,*** 1985, 342 pp.

5 *La dimensión ambiental en los estilos de desarrollo de América Latina, Osvaldo Sunkel*, 1981, 2nd. ed. 1984, 136 pp.

6 *La mujer y el desarrollo: guía para la planificación de programas y proyectos*, 1984, 115 pp.

6 ***Women and development: guidelines for programme and project planning,*** 1982, 3rd. ed. 1984, 123 pp.

7 *África y América Latina: perspectivas de la cooperación interregional*, 1983, 286 pp.

8 Sobrevivencia campesina en ecosistemas de altura, vols. I y II, 1983, 720 pp.

9 La mujer en el sector popular urbano. América Latina y el Caribe, 1984, 349 pp.

10 Avances en la interpretación ambiental del desarrollo agrícola de América Latina, 1985, 236 pp.

11 El decenio de la mujer en el escenario latinoamericano, 1986, 216 pp.

11 **The decade for women in Latin America and the Caribbean: background and prospects,** 1988, 215 pp.

12 América Latina: sistema monetario internacional y financiamiento externo, 1986, 416 pp. (Out of stock)

12 **Latin America: international monetary system and external financing,** 1986, 405 pp. (Out of stock)

13 Raúl Prebisch: Un aporte al estudio de su pensamiento, 1987, 146 pp.

14 Cooperativismo latinoamericano: antecedentes y perspectivas, 1989, 371 pp.

15 CEPAL, 40 años (1948-1988), 1988, 85 pp.

15 **ECLAC 40 Years (1948-1988),** 1989, 83 pp.

16 América Latina en la economía mundial, 1988, 321 pp. (Out of stock)

17 Gestión para el desarrollo de cuencas de alta montaña en la zona andina, 1988, 187 pp.

18 Políticas macroeconómicas y brecha externa: América Latina en los años ochenta, 1989, 201 pp.

19 CEPAL, Bibliografía, 1948-1988, 1989, 648 pp.

20 Desarrollo agrícola y participación campesina, 1989, 404 pp.

21 Planificación y gestión del desarrollo en áreas de expansión de la frontera agropecuaria en América Latina, 1989, 113 pp.

22 Transformación ocupacional y crisis social en América Latina, 1989, 243 pp. (Out of stock)

23 La crisis urbana en América Latina y el Caribe: reflexiones sobre alternativas de solución, 1990, 197 pp. (Out of stock)

24 **The environmental dimension in development planning I,** 1991, 302 pp.

25 Transformación productiva con equidad, 1990, 3rd. ed. 1991, 185 pp.

25 **Changing production patterns with social equity,** 1990, 3rd. ed. 1991, 177 pp.

26 América Latina y el Caribe: opciones para reducir el peso de la deuda, 1990, 118 pp.

26 **Latin America and the Caribbean: options to reduce the debt burden,** 1990, 110 pp.

27 Los grandes cambios y la crisis. Impacto sobre la mujer en América Latina y el Caribe, 1991, 271 pp.

27 **Major changes and crisis. The impact on women in Latin America and the Caribbean,** 1992, 279 pp.

28 **A collection of documents on economic relations between the United States and Central America, 1906-1956,** 1991, 398 pp.

29 Inventarios y cuentas del patrimonio natural en América Latina y el Caribe, 1991, 335 pp.

30 Evaluaciones del impacto ambiental en América Latina y el Caribe, 1991, 232 pp. (Out of stock)

31 El desarrollo sustentable: transformación productiva, equidad y medio ambiente, 1991, 146 pp.

31 **Sustainable development: changing production patterns, social equity and the environment,** 1991, 146 pp.

32 Equidad y transformación productiva: un enfoque integrado, 1993, 254 pp.

33 Educación y conocimiento: eje de la transformación productiva con equidad, 1992, 269 pp.

33 **Education and knowledge: basic pillars of changing production patterns with social equity,** 1993, 257 pp.

34 Ensayos sobre coordinación de políticas macroeconómicas, 1992, 249 pp.

35 Población, equidad y transformación productiva, 1993, 2nd. ed. 1995, 158 pp.

35 **Population, social equity and changing production patterns,** 1993, 153 pp.

36 Cambios en el perfil de las familias. La experiencia regional, 1993, 434 pp.

37 Familia y futuro: un programa regional en América Latina y el Caribe, 1994, 137 pp.

37 **Family and future. A regional programme in Latin America and the Caribbean,** 1995, 123 pp.

38 Imágenes sociales de la modernización y la transformación tecnológica, 1995, 198 pp.

39 El regionalismo abierto en América Latina y el Caribe, 1994, 109 pp.

39 **Open regionalism in Latin America and the Caribbean,** 1994, 103 pp.

40 Políticas para mejorar la inserción en la economía mundial, 1995, 314 pp.

40 **Policies to improve linkages with the global economy,** 1995, 308 pp.

41 Las relaciones económicas entre América Latina y la Unión Europea: el papel de los servicios exteriores, 1996, 300 pp.

42 Fortalecer el desarrollo. Interacciones entre macro y microeconomía, 1996, 116 pp.

42 **Strengthening development. The interplay of macro- and microeconomics,** 1996, 116 pp.

43 Quince años de desempeño económico. América Latina y el Caribe, 1980-1995, 1996, 120 pp.

43 **The economic experience of the last fifteen years. Latin America and the Caribbean, 1980-1995,** 1996, 120 pp.

44 La brecha de la equidad. América Latina, el Caribe y la cumbre social, 1997, 218 pp.

44 **The equity gap. Latin America, the Caribbean and the social summit,** 1997, 219 pp.

45 La grieta de las drogas, 1997, 218 pp.

46 Agroindustria y pequeña agricultura: vínculos, potencialidades y oportunidades comerciales, 1998, 180 pp.

MONOGRAPH SERIES

Cuadernos de la C E P A L

1 *América Latina: el nuevo escenario regional y mundial /Latin America: the new regional and world setting,* (bilingual), 1975, 2nd. ed. 1985, 103 pp.

2 *Las evoluciones regionales de la estrategia internacional del desarrollo,* 1975, 2nd. ed. 1984, 73 pp.

2 *Regional appraisals of the international development strategy,* 1975, 2nd. ed. 1985, 82 pp.

3 *Desarrollo humano, cambio social y crecimiento en América Latina,* 1975, 2nd. ed. 1984, 103 pp.

4 *Relaciones comerciales, crisis monetaria e integración económica en América Latina,* 1975, 85 pp.

5 *Síntesis de la segunda evaluación regional de la estrategia internacional del desarrollo,* 1975, 72 pp.

6 *Dinero de valor constante. Concepto, problemas y experiencias,* Jorge Rose, 1975, 2nd. ed. 1984, 43 pp.

7 *La coyuntura internacional y el sector externo,* 1975, 2nd. ed. 1983, 106 pp.

8 *La industrialización latinoamericana en los años setenta,* 1975, 2nd. ed. 1984, 116 pp.

9 *Dos estudios sobre inflación 1972-1974. La inflación en los países centrales. América Latina y la inflación importada,* 1975, 2nd. ed. 1984, 57 pp.

s/n *Canada and the foreign firm,* D. Pollock, 1976, 43 pp.

10 *Reactivación del mercado común centroamericano,* 1976, 2nd. ed. 1984, 149 pp.

11 *Integración y cooperación entre países en desarrollo en el ámbito agrícola,* Germánico Salgado, 1976, 2nd. ed. 1985, 62 pp.

12 *Temas del nuevo orden económico internacional,* 1976, 2nd. ed. 1984, 85 pp.

13 *En torno a las ideas de la CEPAL: desarrollo, industrialización y comercio exterior,* 1977, 2nd. ed. 1985, 57 pp.

14 *En torno a las ideas de la CEPAL: problemas de la industrialización en América Latina,* 1977, 2nd. ed. 1984, 46 pp.

15 *Los recursos hidráulicos de América Latina. Informe regional,* 1977, 2nd. ed. 1984, 75 pp.

15 *The water resources of Latin America. Regional report,* 1977, 2nd. ed. 1985, 79 pp.

16 *Desarrollo y cambio social en América Latina,* 1977, 2nd. ed. 1984, 59 pp.

17 *Estrategia internacional de desarrollo y establecimiento de un nuevo orden económico internacional,* 1977, 3rd. ed. 1984, 61 pp.

17 *International development strategy and establishment of a new international economic order,* 1977, 3rd. ed. 1985, 59 pp.

18 *Raíces históricas de las estructuras distributivas de América Latina,* A. di Filippo, 1977, 2nd. ed. 1983, 64 pp.

19 *Dos estudios sobre endeudamiento externo,* C. Massad and R. Zahler, 1977, 2nd. ed. 1986, 66 pp.

s/n *United States – Latin American trade and financial relations: some policy recommendations,* S. Weintraub, 1977, 44 pp.

20 *Tendencias y proyecciones a largo plazo del desarrollo económico de América Latina,* 1978, 3rd. ed. 1985, 134 pp.

21 *25 años en la agricultura de América Latina: rasgos principales 1950-1975,* 1978, 2nd. ed. 1983, 124 pp.

22 *Notas sobre la familia como unidad socioeconómica,* Carlos A. Borsotti, 1978, 2nd. ed. 1984, 60 pp.

23 *La organización de la información para la evaluación del desarrollo,* Juan Sourrouille, 1978, 2nd. ed. 1984, 61 pp.

24 *Contabilidad nacional a precios constantes en América Latina,* 1978, 2nd. ed. 1983, 60 pp.

s/n *Energy in Latin America: The Historical Record,* J. Mullen, 1978, 66 pp.

25 *Ecuador: desafíos y logros de la política económica en la fase de expansión petrolera,* 1979, 2nd. ed. 1984, 153 pp.

26 *Las transformaciones rurales en América Latina: ¿desarrollo social o marginación?,* 1979, 2nd. ed. 1984, 160 pp.

27 *La dimensión de la pobreza en América Latina,* Oscar Altimir, 1979, 2nd. ed. 1983, 89 pp. (Out of stock)

28 *Organización institucional para el control y manejo de la deuda externa. El caso chileno,* Rodolfo Hoffman, 1979, 35 pp.

29 *La política monetaria y el ajuste de la balanza de pagos: tres estudios,* 1979, 2nd. ed. 1984, 61 pp.

29 *Monetary policy and balance of payments adjustment: three studies,* 1979, 60 pp. (Out of stock)

30 *América Latina: las evaluaciones regionales de la estrategia internacional del desarrollo en los años setenta,* 1979, 2nd. ed. 1982, 237 pp.

31 *Educación, imágenes y estilos de desarrollo,* G. Rama, 1979, 2nd. ed. 1982, 72 pp.

32 *Movimientos internacionales de capitales,* R. H. Arriazu, 1979, 2nd. ed. 1984, 90 pp.

33 *Informe sobre las inversiones directas extranjeras en América Latina,* A. E. Calcagno, 1980, 2nd. ed. 1982, 114 pp.

34 *Las fluctuaciones de la industria manufacturera argentina, 1950-1978,* D. Heymann, 1980, 2nd. ed. 1984, 234 pp.

35 *Perspectivas de reajuste industrial: la Comunidad Económica Europea y los países en desarrollo,* B. Evers, G. de Groot and W. Wagenmans, 1980, 2nd. ed. 1984, 69 pp.

36 *Un análisis sobre la posibilidad de evaluar la solvencia crediticia de los países en desarrollo,* A. Saieh, 1980, 2nd. ed. 1984, 82 pp.

37 *Hacia los censos latinoamericanos de los años ochenta,* 1981, 146 pp.

s/n *The economic relations of Latin America with Europe,* 1980, 2nd. ed. 1983, 156 pp.

69 **Public Finances in Latin America in the 1980s,** 1993, 96 pp.

70 *Canales, cadenas, corredores y competitividad: un enfoque sistémico y su aplicación a seis productos latinoamericanos de exportación,* 1993, 183 pp.

71 *Focalización y pobreza,* 1995, 249 pp. (Out of stock)

72 *Productividad de los pobres rurales y urbanos,* 1995, 318 pp. (Out of stock)

73 *El gasto social en América Latina: un examen cuantitativo y cualitativo,* 1995, 167 pp.

74 *América Latina y el Caribe: dinámica de la población y desarrollo,* 1995, 151 pp.

75 *Crecimiento de la población y desarrollo,* 1995, 95 pp.

76 *Dinámica de la población y desarrollo económico,* 1997, 116 pp.

77 *La reforma laboral y la participación privada en los puertos del sector público,* 1996, 168 pp.

77 **Labour reform and private participation in public-sector ports,** 1996, 160 pp.

78 *Centroamérica y el TLC: efectos inmediatos e implicaciones futuras,* 1996, 164 pp.

79 *Ciudadanía y derechos humanos desde la perspectiva de las políticas públicas,* 1997, 124 pp.

80 *Evolución del gasto público social en América Latina: 1980-1995,* 1998, 200 pp.

81 *La apertura económica y el desarrollo agrícola en América Latina y el Caribe,* 1997, 136 pp.

82 *A dinámica do Setor Saúde no Brasil,* 1997, 220 pp.

84 *El régimen de contratación petrolera de América Latina en la década de los noventa,* 1998, 134 pp.

Cuadernos Estadísticos de la C E P A L

1 *América Latina: relación de precios del intercambio,* 1976, 2nd. ed. 1984, 66 pp.

2 *Indicadores del desarrollo económico y social en América Latina,* 1976, 2nd. ed. 1984, 179 pp.

3 *Series históricas del crecimiento de América Latina,* 1978, 2nd. ed. 1984, 206 pp.

4 *Estadísticas sobre la estructura del gasto de consumo de los hogares según finalidad del gasto, por grupos de ingreso,* 1978, 110 pp. (Out of print; replaced by No. 8 below)

5 *El balance de pagos de América Latina, 1950-1977,* 1979, 2nd. ed. 1984, 164 pp.

6 *Distribución regional del producto interno bruto sectorial en los países de América Latina,* 1981, 2nd. ed. 1985, 68 pp.

7 *Tablas de insumo-producto en América Latina,* 1983, 383 pp.

8 *Estructura del gasto de consumo de los hogares según finalidad del gasto, por grupos de ingreso,* 1984, 146 pp.

9 *Origen y destino del comercio exterior de los países de la Asociación Latinoamericana de Integración y del Mercado Común Centroamericano,* 1985, 546 pp.

10 *América Latina: balance de pagos, 1950-1984,* 1986, 357 pp.

11 *El comercio exterior de bienes de capital en América Latina,* 1986, 288 pp.

12 *América Latina: índices del comercio exterior, 1970-1984,* 1987, 355 pp.

13 *América Latina: comercio exterior según la clasificación industrial internacional uniforme de todas las actividades económicas,* 1987, Vol. I, 675 pp; Vol. II, 675 pp.

14 *La distribución del ingreso en Colombia. Antecedentes estadísticos y características socioeconómicas de los receptores,* 1988, 156 pp.

15 *América Latina y el Caribe: series regionales de cuentas nacionales a precios constantes de 1980,* 1991, 245 pp.

16 *Origen y destino del comercio exterior de los países de la Asoción Latinoamericana de Integración,* 1991, 190 pp.

17 *Comercio intrazonal de los países de la Asociación de Integración, según capítulos de la clasificación uniforme para el comercio internacional, revisión 2,* 1992, 299 pp.

18 *Clasificaciones estadísticas internacionales incorporadas en el Banco de Datos del Comercio Exterior de América Latina y el Caribe de la CEPAL,* 1993, 313 pp.

19 *América Latina: comercio exterior según la clasificación industrial internacional uniforme de todas las actividades económicas (CIIU) - Volumen I -Exportaciones,* 1993, 285 pp.

19 *América Latina: comercio exterior según la clasificación industrial internacional uniforme de todas las actividades económicas (CIIU) - Volumen II -Importaciones,* 1993, 291 pp.

20 *Dirección del comercio exterior de América Latina y el Caribe según principales productos y grupos de productos, 1970-1992,* 1994, 483 pp.

21 *Estructura del gasto de consumo de los hogares en América Latina,* 1995, 274 pp.

22 *América Latina y el Caribe: dirección del comercio exterior de los principales productos alimenticios y agrícolas según países de destino y procedencia, 1979-1993,* 1995, 224 pp.

23 *América Latina y el Caribe: series regionales y oficiales de cuentas nacionales, 1950-1994,* 1996, 130 pp.

24 *Chile: comercio exterior según grupos de la Clasificación Uniforme para el Comercio Internacional, Rev. 3, y países de destino y procedencia, 1990-1995,* 1996, 480 pp.

25 *Clasificaciones estadísticas internacionales incorporadas en el Banco de Datos del Comercio Exterior de América Latina y el Caribe de la CEPAL,* 1998, 287 pp.

26 *América Latina y el Caribe: series estadísticas sobre comercio de servicios 1980-1997,* 1998, 124 pp.

Estudios e Informes de la C E P A L

1   *Nicaragua: el impacto de la mutación política*, 1981, 2nd. ed. 1982, 126 pp.

2   *Perú 1968-1977: la política económica en un proceso de cambio global*, 1981, 2nd. ed. 1982, 166 pp.

3   *La industrialización de América Latina y la cooperación internacional*, 1981, 170 pp. (Out of print, will not be reprinted.)

4   *Estilos de desarrollo, modernización y medio ambiente en la agricultura latinoamericana*, 1981, 4th. ed. 1984, 130 pp.

5   *El desarrollo de América Latina en los años ochenta*, 1981, 2nd. ed. 1982, 153 pp.

5   **Latin American development in the 1980s,** 1981, 2nd. ed. 1982, 134 pp.

6   *Proyecciones del desarrollo latinoamericano en los años ochenta*, 1981, 3rd. ed. 1985, 96 pp.

6   **Latin American development projections for the 1980s,** 1982, 2nd. ed. 1983, 89 pp.

7   *Las relaciones económicas externas de América Latina en los años ochenta*, 1981, 2nd. ed. 1982, 180 pp. (Out of stock)

8   *Integración y cooperación regionales en los años ochenta*, 1982, 2nd. ed. 1982, 174 pp.

9   *Estrategias de desarrollo sectorial para los años ochenta: industria y agricultura*, 1981, 2nd. ed. 1985, 100 pp.

10 *Dinámica del subempleo en América Latina. PREALC*, 1981, 2nd. ed. 1985, 101 pp.

11 *Estilos de desarrollo de la industria manufacturera y medio ambiente en América Latina*, 1982, 2nd. ed. 1984, 178 pp.

12 *Relaciones económicas de América Latina con los países miembros del "Consejo de Asistencia Mutua Económica"*, 1982, 154 pp.

13 *Campesinado y desarrollo agrícola en Bolivia*, 1982, 175 pp.

14 *El sector externo: indicadores y análisis de sus fluctuaciones. El caso argentino*, 1982, 2nd. ed. 1985, 216 pp.

15 *Ingeniería y consultoría en Brasil y el Grupo Andino*, 1982, 320 pp.

16 *Cinco estudios sobre la situación de la mujer en América Latina*, 1982, 2nd. ed. 1985, 178 pp.

16 **Five studies on the situation of women in Latin America,** 1983, 2nd. ed. 1984, 188 pp.

17 *Cuentas nacionales y producto material en América Latina*, 1982, 129 pp.

18 *El financiamiento de las exportaciones en América Latina*, 1983, 212 pp.

19 *Medición del empleo y de los ingresos rurales*, 1982, 2nd. ed. 1983, 173 pp.

19 **Measurement of employment and income in rural areas,** 1983, 184 pp.

20 *Efectos macroeconómicos de cambios en las barreras al comercio y al movimiento de capitales: un modelo de simulación*, 1982, 68 pp. (Out of stock)

21 *La empresa pública en la economía: la experiencia argentina*, 1982, 2nd. ed. 1985, 134 pp.

22 *Las empresas transnacionales en la economía de Chile, 1974-1980*, 1983, 178 pp.

23 *La gestión y la informática en las empresas ferroviarias de América Latina y España*, 1983, 195 pp.

24 *Establecimiento de empresas de reparación y mantenimiento de contenedores en América Latina y el Caribe*, 1983, 314 pp.

24 **Establishing container repair and maintenance enterprises in Latin America and the Caribbean,** 1983, 236 pp.

25 *Agua potable y saneamiento ambiental en América Latina, 1981-1990 / Drinking water supply and sanitation in Latin America, 1981-1990* (bilingual), 1983, 140 pp.

26 *Los bancos transnacionales, el estado y el endeudamiento externo en Bolivia*, 1983, 282 pp.

27 *Política económica y procesos de desarrollo. La experiencia argentina entre 1976 y 1981*, 1983, 157 pp.

28 *Estilos de desarrollo, energía y medio ambiente: un estudio de caso exploratorio*, 1983, 129 pp.

29 *Empresas transnacionales en la industria de alimentos. El caso argentino: cereales y carne*, 1983, 93 pp.

30 *Industrialización en Centroamérica, 1960-1980*, 1983, 168 pp.

31 *Dos estudios sobre empresas transnacionales en Brasil*, 1983, 141 pp.

32 *La crisis económica internacional y su repercusión en América Latina*, 1983, 81 pp.

33 *La agricultura campesina en sus relaciones con la industria*, 1984, 120 pp.

34 *Cooperación económica entre Brasil y el Grupo Andino: el caso de los minerales y metales no ferrosos*, 1983, 148 pp.

35 *La agricultura campesina y el mercado de alimentos: la dependencia externa y sus efectos en una economía abierta*, 1984, 201 pp.

36 *El capital extranjero en la economía peruana*, 1984, 178 pp.

37 *Dos estudios sobre política arancelaria*, 1984, 96 pp.

38 *Estabilización y liberalización económica en el Cono Sur*, 1984, 193 pp.

39 *La agricultura campesina y el mercado de alimentos: el caso de Haití y el de la República Dominicana*, 1984, 255 pp.

40 *La industria siderúrgica latinoamericana: tendencias y potencial*, 1984, 280 pp.

41 *La presencia de las empresas transnacionales en la economía ecuatoriana*, 1984, 77 pp.

42 *Precios, salarios y empleo en la Argentina: estadísticas económicas de corto plazo*, 1984, 378 pp.

43 El desarrollo de la seguridad social en América Latina, 1985, 348 pp.

44 Market structure, firm size and Brazilian exports, 1985, 104 pp.

45 La planificación del transporte en países de América Latina, 1985, 247 pp.

46 La crisis en América Latina: su evaluación y perspectivas, 1985, 119 pp.

47 La juventud en América Latina y el Caribe, 1985, 181 pp.

48 Desarrollo de los recursos mineros de América Latina, 1985, 145 pp.

48 Development of the mining resources of Latin America, 1989, 160 pp.

49 Las relaciones económicas internacionales de América Latina y la cooperación regional, 1985, 224 pp.

50 América Latina y la economía mundial del algodón, 1985, 122 pp.

51 Comercio y cooperación entre países de América Latina y países miembros del CAME, 1985, 90 pp.

52 Trade relations between Brazil and the United States, 1985, 148 pp. (Out of stock)

53 Los recursos hídricos de América Latina y el Caribe y su aprovechamiento, 1985, 138 pp.

53 The water resources of Latin America and the Caribbean and their utilization, 1985, 135 pp.

54 La pobreza en América Latina: dimensiones y políticas, 1985, 155 pp.

55 Políticas de promoción de exportaciones en algunos países de América Latina, 1985, 207 pp.

56 Las empresas transnacionales en la Argentina, 1986, 222 pp.

57 El desarrollo frutícola y forestal en Chile y sus derivaciones sociales, 1986, 227 pp.

58 El cultivo del algodón y la soya en el Paraguay y sus derivaciones sociales, 1986, 141 pp.

59 Expansión del cultivo de la caña de azúcar y de la ganadería en el nordeste del Brasil: un examen del papel de la política pública y de sus derivaciones económicas y sociales, 1986, 164 pp.

60 Las empresas transnacionales en el desarrollo colombiano, 1986, 212 pp.

61 Las empresas transnacionales en la economía del Paraguay, 1987, 115 pp.

62 Problemas de la industria latinoamericana en la fase crítica, 1986, 113 pp.

63 Relaciones económicas internacionales y cooperación regional de América Latina y el Caribe, 1987, 272 pp.

63 International economic relations and regional co-operation in Latin America and the Caribbean, 1987, 267 pp.

64 Tres ensayos sobre inflación y políticas de estabilización, 1986, 201 pp.

65 La industria farmacéutica y farmoquímica: desarrollo histórico y posibilidades futuras. Argentina, Brasil y México, 1987, 177 pp.

66 Dos estudios sobre América Latina y el Caribe y la economía internacional, 1987, 125 pp.

67 Reestructuración de la industria automotriz mundial y perspectivas para América Latina, 1987, 232 pp.

68 Cooperación latinoamericana en servicios: antecedentes y perspectivas, 1988, 155 pp.

69 Desarrollo y transformación: estrategia para superar la pobreza, 1988, 114 pp.

69 Development and change: strategies for vanquishing poverty, 1988, 114 pp.

70 La evolución económica del Japón y su impacto en América Latina, 1988, 88 pp.

70 The economic evolution of Japan and its impact on Latin America, 1990, 79 pp.

71 La gestión de los recursos hídricos en América Latina y el Caribe, 1989, 256 pp.

72 La evolución del problema de la deuda externa en América Latina y el Caribe, 1988, 77 pp.

72 The evolution of the external debt problem in Latin America and the Caribbean, 1988, 69 pp.

73 Agricultura, comercio exterior y cooperación internacional, 1988, 83 pp.

73 Agriculture, external trade and international co-operation, 1989, 79 pp.

74 Reestructuración industrial y cambio tecnológico: consecuencias para América Latina, 1989, 105 pp.

75 El medio ambiente como factor de desarrollo, 1989, 2nd. ed. 1991, 123 pp.

76 El comportamiento de los bancos transnacionales y la crisis internacional de endeudamiento, 1989, 214 pp.

76 Transnational bank behaviour and the international debt crisis, 1989, 198 pp.

77 Los recursos hídricos de América Latina y del Caribe: planificación, desastres naturales y contaminación, 1990, 266 pp.

77 The water resources of Latin America and the Caribbean - Planning hazards and pollution, 1990, 252 pp.

78 La apertura financiera en Chile y el comportamiento de los bancos transnacionales, 1990, 132 pp.

79 La industria de bienes de capital en América Latina y el Caribe: su desarrollo en un marco de cooperación regional, 1991, 235 pp.

80 Impacto ambiental de la contaminación hídrica producida por la Refinería Estatal Esmeraldas: análisis técnico-económico, 1991, 189 pp.

81 Magnitud de la pobreza en América Latina en los años ochenta, 1991, 177 pp.

82 América Latina y el Caribe: el manejo de la escasez de agua, 1991, 148 pp.

83 Reestructuración y desarrollo de la industria automotriz mexicana en los años ochenta: evolución y perspectivas, 1992, 191 pp.

84 La transformación de la producción en Chile: cuatro ensayos de interpretación, 1993, 372 pp.

85 *Inversión extranjera y empresas transnacionales en la economía de Chile (1974-1989). Proyectos de inversión y estrategias de las empresas transnacionales,* 1992, 257 pp.

86 *Inversión extranjera y empresas transnacionales en la economía de Chile (1974-1989). El papel del capital extranjero y la estrategia nacional de desarrollo,* 1992, 163 pp.

87 *Análisis de cadenas agroindustriales en Ecuador y Perú,* 1993, 294 pp.

88 *El comercio de manufacturas de América Latina. Evolución y estructura 1962-1989,* 1993, 150, pp.

89 *El impacto económico y social de las migraciones en Centroamérica,* 1993, 78 pp.

90 *El papel de las empresas transnacionales en la reestructuración industrial de Colombia: una síntesis,* 1993, 131 pp.

91 *Las empresas transnacionales de una economía en transición: La experiencia argentina en los años ochenta,* 1995, 193 pp.

92 *Reestructuración y desarrollo productivo: desafío y potencial para los años noventa,* 1994, 108 pp.

93 *Comercio internacional y medio ambiente. La discusión actual,* 1995, 112 pp. (Out of stock)

94 *Innovación en tecnologías y sistemas de gestión ambientales en empresas líderes latinoamericanas,* 1995, 206 pp.

95 *México: la industria maquiladora,* 1996, 237 pp.

Serie INFOPLAN: Temas Especiales del Desarrollo

1 *Resúmenes de documentos sobre deuda externa,* 1986, 324 pp.

2 *Resúmenes de documentos sobre cooperación entre países en desarrollo,* 1986, 189 pp.

3 *Resúmenes de documentos sobre recursos hídricos,* 1987, 290 pp.

4 *Resúmenes de documentos sobre planificación y medio ambiente,* 1987, 111 pp.

5 *Resúmenes de documentos sobre integración económica en América Latina y el Caribe,* 1987, 273 pp.

6 *Resúmenes de documentos sobre cooperación entre países en desarrollo, II parte,* 1988, 146 pp.

7 *Documentos sobre privatización con énfasis en América Latina,* 1991, 82 pp.

8 *Reseñas de documentos sobre desarrollo ambientalmente sustentable,* 1992, 217 pp. (Out of stock)

9 *MERCOSUR: resúmenes de documentos,* 1993, 119 pp.

10 *Políticas sociales: resúmenes de documentos,* 1995, 95 pp.

11 *Modernización del Estado: resúmenes de documentos,* 1995, 73 pp.

12 *Gestión de la información: reseñas de documentos,* 1996, 152 pp.

13 *Políticas sociales: resúmenes de documentos II,* 1997, 80 pp.

Recent co-publications

On occasion ECLAC concludes agreements for the co-publication of texts that may be of special interest to other international organizations or to publishing houses. In the latter case, the publishing houses have exclusive sales and distribution rights.

Las nuevas corrientes financieras hacia América Latina: Fuentes, efectos y políticas, Ricardo Ffrench-Davis y Stephany Griffith-Jones (comp.), México, CEPAL/ Fondo de Cultura Económica, primera edición, 1995.

Hacia un nuevo modelo de organización mundial. El sector manufacturero argentino en los años noventa. Jorge Katz, Roberto Bisang, Gustavo Burachick editores, CEPAL/IDRC/Alianza Editorial, Buenos Aires, 1996.

América Latina y el Caribe quince años después. De la década perdida a la transformación económica 1980-1995, CEPAL/Fondo de Cultura Económica. Santiago, 1996.

Flujos de Capital e Inversión Productiva. Lecciones para América Latina, Ricardo Ffrench-Davis -Helmut Reisen (compiladores). CEPAL/M. Graw Hill, Santiago, 1997.

Políticas para mejorar la inserción en la economía mundial. América y El Caribe, CEPAL/Fondo de Cultura Económica. Santiago, 1997.

La Economía Cubana. Reformas estructurales y desempeño en los noventa, Comisión Económica para América Latina y el Caribe. CEPAL/Fondo de Cultura Económica, México, 1997.

La Igualdad de los Modernos: reflexiones acerca de la realización de los derechos económicos, sociales y culturales en América Latina, CEPAL/IIDH, Costa Rica, 1997.

Estrategias empresariales en tiempos de cambio, Bernardo Kosacoff (editor), CEPAL/Universidad Nacional de Quilmes, Argentina, 1998.

Grandes empresas y grupos industriales latinoamericanos, Wilson Peres (coord.), CEPAL/XXI Siglo veintiuno editores, Buenos Aires, 1998.

Cincuenta años de pensamiento en la CEPAL: textos seleccionados, dos volúmenes, CEPAL/Fondo de Cultura Económica, Santiago, 1998.